Hermano

¡Qué plac

Espíritu Santo!   ¡Gracias por su
                     ministerio!
                      Octavio
                       Esqueda

# ANOINTED
# TEACHING

*Partnership with the Holy Spirit*

# Robert W. Pazmiño
# Octavio J. Esqueda

PUBLICACIONES
**KERIGMA**
Εν αρχή ήν ο λόγος

© 2019 Publicaciones Kerigma
Salem Oregón, Estados Unidos
http://www.publicacioneskerigma.org

**Diseño de Portada:** Publicaciones Kerigma

2019 Publicaciones Kerigma
Salem Oregón
All rights reserved

Pedidos: 971 304-1735

www.publicacioneskerigma.org

ISBN: 978-1-948578-23-3

*Impreso en Estados Unidos*

*Printed in United States*

"A valuable discussion that will allow the reader better to understand on the one hand the educational task of the church, and on the other the role of the Spirit in that task. In this encounter between pneumatology and education, firmly grounded on Scripture, both are widened and strengthened."

**Dr. Justo L. González**
**Historian, educator, and prolific theological writer**

"Discover the Holy Spirit and its work in new ways as you read these pages. The authors include new perspectives and dimensions of the Holy Spirit as it relates to Christian education that refresh and inspire our work and commitments as educators of the church. The integration of the biblical/theological with the practice and theory of Christian education is not found in other sources like you will find here. The reading is accessible for scholars, as well as lay teachers while accessibility has not substituted depth of thought."

**Dr. Elizabeth Conde Frazier, Coordinator of Relations for Theological Institutions, Association for Hispanic Theological Education**

"Anointed teaching produces clear, deep and transforming results! Robert Pazmiño and Octavio Esqueda invite us to partner with the Holy Spirit to produce liberation, celebration, sustenance, and the fruit of the Spirit with our teaching. They engage the Scriptures and the thoughts of educators and change agents to demonstrate that our task as teachers is to focus on the transforming impact that the Holy Spirit wants to produce in human beings. This book invites us to combine an updated pedagogy with the Holy Spirit power to join God in his work in individuals and society through his Spirit. We urgently need this transformative vision for the educational task. We are thankful to the authors for presenting it."

**Dr. Juan Martínez**
**Professor of Hispanic Studies and Pastoral Leadership, Fuller Theological Seminary**

"For many educators, "pneumatology" and "pedagogy" are not usually go-to words for describing education that is Christian. Yet Jesus promised that the teacher of his followers would be the Holy Spirit. And recognizing the neglected place of the Spirit in most Christian traditions' training efforts, Robert W. Pazmiño and Octavio J. Esqueda explore Spirit-infused education in their book *Anointed Teaching: Partnership with the Holy Spirit*. These respected experts draw on broad international experience and a wide range of sources— geographically, across time, and inclusive of the main branches of Christianity—for helping teachers embrace and pass on Spirit-filled faith. Highly recommended."

**Dr. Sandra Glahn, Dallas Theological Seminary professor and author of more than twenty-five books, including the Coffee Cup Bible Study series**

"I love it when another good foundational book comes out to stir our thinking about faithful and effective educational ministry in the church. *Anointed Teaching: Partnership with the Holy Spirit,* is a welcome new text about what it means to teach and preach the Bible with the Holy Spirit in ways that God can use to form His people in their inner spiritual lives and their outer expressions of faithful living. Pazmiño and Esqueda have offered us thoughtful reflection on what teaching with the Spirit should be like in light of themes they see flowing from our baptism as followers of Christ ("liberation"), our participation in receiving the Lord's Supper ("celebration"), and the giving of the Spirit at Pentecost ("sustenance"). Like Pazmiño's earlier works that explored the teaching ministry of the church in light of the Father's teaching work in and for us (*God Our Teacher: Theological Basics in Christian Education*) and Jesus' teaching ministry example (*So What Makes Our Teaching Christian? Teaching in the Name, Spirit and Power of Jesus*), this book on the ongoing teaching ministry of the Holy Spirit invites us to consider carefully what it means to partner with God in teaching that becomes transformative inside and out. I love being challenged by good friends and this text gives me much to consider as I strive to be faithful in my teaching ministries."

**Dr. Kevin E. Lawson, Professor of Educational Studies at Talbot School of Theology, Biola University, and Editor of the *Christian Education Journal***

"Anointing teaching focuses on the cooperative work of the teacher, informed by the best in social science, while placing dependency on the liberative power of third person of the Triune God---the Holy Spirit. Pazmiño and Esqueda's book gives focus to the Holy Spirit's revelation and empowerment to transform human persons into Christlike disciples through faithful teaching."

**Mark A. Maddix, Dean**
**School of Theology & Christian Ministry**
**Point Loma Nazarene University**

"This is not a how-to book on teaching, but one with the daring vision that Christian teaching is a vocation, a high calling, which is empowered by God's Spirit, embodies the gifts of the Spirit, and generates the transformative life-giving fruits of the Spirit. Teaching requires a prophetic and participatory pneumatology whose mission is to touch every dimension of individual, community, and social existence. Teaching is a profound privilege and a responsibility! This volume explains why. "

**Dr. M. Daniel Carroll R. (Rodas)**
**Blanchard Professor of Old Testament Wheaton College and Graduate School**

# TABLE OF CONTENTS

*To all our students,*
*past, present and future*
*and*
*To our wives, Wanda and Angélica,*
*partners in life and ministry*

# Introduction

This work completes a theological trilogy that explores the essential elements of Christian teaching. The first volume, *God Our Teacher: Theological Basics in Christian Education* encouraged Christian teachers to be theocentric in their ministries honoring their relationship with a God who is for, despite, with, in, through and beyond us in life and ministry. The second volume entitled *So What Makes Our Teaching Christian? Teaching in the Name, Spirit and Power of Jesus* encouraged Christian teachers to be Christocentric in their ministries as followers, disciples and friends of Jesus representing him and conforming to his mind and example.

This third volume, *Anointed Teaching: Partnership with the Holy Spirit* encourages Christian teachers to be pneumatocentric in their ministries working in partnership with the Holy Spirit and bearing fruits of liberation, celebration, and sustenance in a world desperate for genuine spiritual life and transformation. Whereas the first two volumes of this theological trilogy were written by one author, this third volume by serendipity and necessity is co-authored by two authors noting the essential role of partnership in ministry anointed by the Holy Spirit and following Jesus' pattern of sending out his disciples in pairs.

How is it possible to be theocentric, Christocentric and pneumatocentric all at the same time as Christian teachers? In an age of multitasking this is a real possibility, but actually the second century church father Irenaeus helps us to handle this challenge in the third millennium. As Irenaeus explored his understanding of the trinity in his time, he suggested that God has two hands operative in God's ministries in all creation. Those two hands are the Word or Christ and the Spirit. While recognizing the limits of anthropological thinking, our two-handed triune God is revealed as always working in partnership with both God the Son and God the Spirit in creation, redemption and consummation. In a similar way we as Christian teachers are called to always work in partnership with the Holy Spirit in bearing the real fruits of liberation, celebration, and sustenance in teaching today.

Partnership with the Holy Spirit always requires various forms of partnership with colleagues in actual ministry settings. While attending a professional conference of the Society of Professors of Christian Education, formerly North American Professors of Christian Education in Dallas, Texas during October 2012, Robert (Bob) Pazmiño was approached by Octavio Esqueda from Talbot Theological Seminary and Steve Kang then from Gordon-Conwell Theological seminary inquiring about the possibility of cooperating on a collaborative work together given our collegial relationship over the years. Bob shared with them a copy of the book proposal entitled *Anointed Teaching*. Both expressed great interest in collaborating on that work. Steve due to extended family needs could not commit time to this project, but Octavio and Bob were able to form the professional partnership that undergirds this work. Partnerships develop in amazing ways in Christian ministries.

Jesus was wise in sending out his disciples in twos and this work honors the partnership the Holy Spirit navigated in the inception of this two-handed work that also honors the host of persons who make such a publication possible.

The general objectives of this book are threefold and include:

1. To explore the biblical and theological distinctive elements of Christian teaching in relation to the person and work of the Holy Spirit.
2. To reaffirm the importance of teaching and God's blessings of liberation, celebration, and sustenance to guide teaching ministries in a variety of settings globally.
3. To inspire Christians in relation to their calling to teach with its expected fruits.

Serendipitously, the two authors of this work share Hispanic roots and generational differences. Octavio is a first-generation scholar with roots from Mexico. Bob is a third-generation scholar with roots on his father's side from Ecuador. Therefore, this work implicitly honors a multi-generational perspective on the ministry of the Holy Spirit who seeks to bless all generations with anointed teaching bearing the fruits of liberation, celebration, and sustenance.

CHAPTER 1

# Theological Basics

Robert W. Pazmiño
Octavio J. Esqueda

In exploring the person and ministry of the Holy Spirit in Christian teaching and learning, we are drawn to the biblical accounts that affirm the Spirit's presence in all of life. Christians have rightfully stressed the key role of redemption made possible in Jesus Christ for those who follow him, yet the Spirit's work encompasses creation prior to redemption, and God's plans for consummation at the end of the age. This chapter gives its primary focus on the Spirit's ministry through redemption bookended with consideration of both creation and consummation for understanding our partnership with the Holy Spirit in all of life from its beginning to end.

## Creation

From the very beginnings of creation accounts, God's Spirit, described as a mighty wind, is moving across the face of the waters (Gen 1:3). Light and darkness emerge from the chaos along with morning and evening the first day. The Spirit's presence is evident in discerning differences and calling forth order and life, form and freedom, as God speaks the universe into existence. Genesis 1:26 describes the creation of humankind: "Let us make humankind in our image, according to our likeness." Part of the human likeness to God that Christians affirm, implies the work of the Trinity (Creator, Son and Spirit) with the designation of "us" and "our likeness or image" in the text, and includes a spiritual dimension that enables communion of the human spirit with God's Spirit, the Holy Spirit. Genesis 2:7 provides yet another account that focuses upon human creation: "then the Lord God formed man from the dust of the ground, and breathed into his nostrils the breath of life; and the man became a living being." The Spirit's presence as *ruah*, the very breath of life, enables humans to be living beings with the freedom of choice to honor their Creator or to opt for immersion in creation without a relationship with God at the center of their existence.

Honoring a partnership with the Spirit for the full realization of life and reflecting God's image and likeness in their ministries, Christian teachers are dealing with a practical pneumatology. A practical pneumatology deals with our understanding of God's Spirit, the Holy Spirit in relation to our actual lives and our teaching ministries and practices. In sustaining a relationship with the Holy Spirit, these ministries imply a practical pneumatology, an understanding of the person and work of Holy Spirit with implications for the practices of teaching and learning.

While each chapter of this work explores theological basics and connections, this chapter directly proposes a practical pneumatology. This chapter considers how the Spirit's legacy is played out in the ministries of Jesus' followers, in particular the ministries of teaching and learning across the life span. Two corresponding questions emerge in relation to this chapter: How was the Spirit involved in teaching ministries in the biblical record (the Holy Spirit as teacher)? What is possible for Christians today in their teaching ministries guided, empowered and filled with the Holy Spirit (our involvement in the teaching ministries of the Spirit with our endowed gifts of teaching)?

In relation to each of the three parts of this work we propose a theological category that helps to both ground and launch consideration of the Christian ministry of teaching. First, in relation to teaching filled with the Spirit, liberation looms prominent in affirming a sense of Baptismal identity. Baptismal identity embraces salvation and Christian freedom as God intended from the very first breathing of life into Adam and Eve. One's Christian identity centers in one's adoption as a child of God and one's calling as a follower of Jesus symbolized through one's baptism and the liberation it embraces in all of life. Second, in relation to teaching in the Spirit, the celebration of Christian virtues emerges in affirming one's Eucharistic identity and the table fellowship shared by Christian teachers and students alike. The virtues that shape Christian character require a daily partnership with and partaking of the Spirit to guide our living, loving and even dying. It is possible to define teaching as showing how to live, love and die in partnership with the Holy Spirit.[1] Third, in relation to sustained teaching, our Pentecostal identity and calling provides a model for guiding how Christian teachers consider the possibility of renewal and transformation in their ministries and in the lives of their students and their wider communities. Thus, the three spiritual fruits of anointed teaching are liberation, celebration, and

---

[1] See Gabriel Moran, *Showing How: The Act of Teaching* (Valley Forge, PA: Trinity, 1997), 39 who suggests "to teach is to show how to live and how to die." I think the addition of "to love" is crucial in Christian faith.

sustenance. Therefore, the Baptismal, Eucharistic and Pentecostal identities of Christians made possible in Jesus Christ provide three touchstones for teaching in partnership with the Holy Spirit. These touchstones for Christian teaching provide a sense of calling, a model for service and an embrace of liberation that Jesus himself modeled in the inauguration of his own teaching ministry described in Luke 4:16-30 that paradoxically included his rejection at Nazareth, his hometown.

In his first public teaching while launching his Galilean ministry it is noted: "Then Jesus filled with the power of the Spirit, returned to Galilee, and a report spread through all the surrounding country. He began to teach in their synagogues and was praised by everyone." (Luke 4:14-15) In his home town of Nazareth on the Sabbath and in the synagogue, he read from Isaiah 61:1, 2:

> The Spirit of the Lord is upon me, because he has anointed me to bring good news to the poor. He has sent me to proclaim release to the captives and the recovery of sight to the blind, and to let the oppressed go free, to proclaim the year of the Lord's favor. (Luke 4: 18-19)

Isaiah described the good tidings of salvation proclaimed to all humanity. Jesus, the anointed one, launches his public teaching ministry with the theme of liberation that is not well received by those who knew him well. It offended them to the point of rage. Their anger leads to their attempt to kill him. Luke positions Jesus' first public anointed teaching after accounts of his baptism and his temptation in the wilderness that brings opposition in various forms to his clear message of good news.

## Baptismal Calling: Liberation

Being baptized as a follower of Jesus Christ involves baptism with the Holy Spirit and fire as John the Baptist described it (Matt 3:11) as compared with John's own ministry with water. Jesus' own baptism was with water and the Spirit symbolized in the form of a dove (Matt 3:13-17). With such a baptism of their own, Christian teachers embrace the teaching role of the Spirit and the liberation it offers in Jesus Christ. Being baptized in Jesus' name and following his example requires identification with the salvation he offers for the past, present and future of our lives. The "fire" in teaching following Jesus' example I relate to the insights of Augustine of North Africa who suggested that "one loving spirit sets another on fire."[2] Teaching in the spirit of Jesus requires compassion and service and raises the matter of the essential ethos of his

---

[2] Augustine of Hippo, *Confessions*, Book IV, chapter 14, paragraph 21.

teaching as described in Luke's account. This ethos, referring to the tone or quality of Jesus' teaching, modeled a moment-to-moment reliance upon God in response to human need guided by love for humankind and their full liberation. Jesus' love eventuated in the shedding of his blood and the giving of his body upon the cross. This compassionate service is recalled in the repeated celebration of his table fellowship in the Christian community. Teaching in the spirit of Jesus calls for welcoming others, calls for learning, sharing, and worshipping with them with the goal of their liberation. What is meant by liberation? It is the full salvation God intends for humanity and all of creation that embraces all of life, personal, communal and corporate life associated with the Hebrew word *shalom* that includes both justice and peace.

The promise of the crucifixion and its efficacy is realized in Jesus' resurrection. Resurrection follows from the crucifixion. Resurrection cannot be separated from the reality of the cross and what God's love accomplished through Jesus' life and death. The cross and Jesus' crucifixion remains a memorial for the extent of love that Jesus calls his followers to consider in their teaching ministries. Believers' baptism identifies with the death and resurrection of Jesus Christ. The Book of Hebrews describes this reality in Hebrews 12:2; "looking to Jesus the pioneer and perfecter of our faith, who for the sake of the joy that was set before him endured the cross, disregarding its shame, and has taken his seat at the right hand of the throne of God." Near the front door to my home, a plaque is set on one side of the wall that displays a cross with the word "joy" emblazed under it. The joy set before Jesus finds expression in his resurrection that makes possible our liberation. Liberation is one of the first fruits of anointed teaching in the twenty-first century just as it was in Jesus' first century ministry.

## Eucharistic Calling: Celebration

By teaching in the Spirit of Jesus, Christians serve in a representative fashion their Lord and Savior that is nurtured through their table fellowship that memorializes his life, death and resurrection. The pattern of table fellowship is repeated in Luke's Gospel with the encounter on the road to Emmaus (Luke 24:13-35). The first miracle at the wedding feast in Cana sets the pattern that is prominent in the crucifixion and renewed in the shared meal on the road waiting the final fulfillment of the marriage supper of the lamb described in the Book of Revelation (Rev 19:1-10). Christians reenact this table fellowship when they celebrate the Lord's Supper and I suggest whenever Christian teachers share the fruits of learning with others in the spirit and name of Jesus.

This suggests that teaching itself and the accompanying learning are sacramental acts in the sense of being a means of God's grace gifted to humanity. This is the fruit of celebration in anointed teaching. Christians bear the name of Christ. They embrace as followers those virtues and values that typified the teaching ministry and life of Jesus. Christian virtues or values need to be incarnated in their own teaching practices by the work of the Holy Spirit working in partnership with human spirits. Christian virtues need to be celebrated by the work of the Holy Spirit with a freedom for truth, love, faith, hope and joy experienced in human life. This celebration honors the gifts of the Spirit served up for human consumption and delight.

## Celebration of Christian Virtues

God's grace in Jesus finds expression in the Christian virtues of faith, hope, love, truth and joy. These five virtues of truth, faith, hope, love and joy capture what Christian teachers are called to incarnate in their teaching ministries to faithfully represent their identity as followers of Jesus with gifts of the Spirit empowering their ministries. By assuming the name of Jesus and following him as disciples and receiving the Spirit, Christian teachers strive for embodiment or living out those virtues that best characterized Jesus and therefore represent his essential character. Christian teachers, given their real limitations and sins, do not fully exemplify Jesus in their individual ministries, but they hold the potential in their corporate expressions to be identified as the Body of Christ as well God's children (daughters and sons) and a household of the Spirit.

As a household of the Spirit, Christians through diverse teaching ministries historically and globally bring glory and honor to the name of Jesus in their Eucharistic calling. They can also dishonor Jesus' name and squelch the Spirit in their efforts.

While teaching in a representative fashion in Jesus' name and imbibing the Spirit, Christians recognize ways in which their actual practices fail to embody Christian virtues. Both personal practices and corporate designs and structures may fail to uphold the name of Jesus and detract from the ideals incarnated in his ministry. The naming of these real gaps and the confession of sin by persons and those who represent structures and associations are necessary for the possibility of more faithful expressions in the present and future. The recognition of the need for change and transformation is also a matter of Jesus' prophetic tradition of teaching. To fulfill God's purposes in teaching, learning and living, reliance upon the Holy Spirit is essential.

Christian teachers are to represent the very life and Spirit of Jesus in their persons and teaching practices. This is a high calling and worthy of the most diligent and receptive of Christians to abide in Christ as Christ graciously abides by his Spirit in the lives of believers. This reality fulfills Jesus' prayer as recorded in John 17:20-23:

> As you, Father, are in me and I in you, may they also be in us, so that the world may believe that you have sent me. The glory that you have given me I have given them, so that they may be one, as we are one, I in them and you in me, that they may become completely one, so that the world may know that you have sent me and have loved them even as you have loved me.

This amazing paradox is also a glorious one where Jesus is made present through the faithful teaching ministries of his disciples in a representative way. In this process Christian teachers recognize the gaps, dysfunctions and discrepancies in their own lives and ministries. Nevertheless, at their best, Christian teachers rely upon the Spirit of Jesus Christ to correct and transcend those gaps, known theologically as sin, in order to represent the living Spirit of Christ in their ministries. Reliance upon the Word and the Spirit is essential.

Christian teachers' strivings to be filled by the Spirit are complemented by reliance upon God's gracious working within them by the Spirit to accomplish divine purposes, a living partnership. This divine working embraces the paradoxes of life and death and both divine and human efforts with their roots in the incarnation.

Christian teachers are privileged to have access to the all that the triune God intends for humanity with God as the educator of all creation, Jesus as the exemplar for teaching practice and the Holy Spirit as ever-present partner in one's calling to teach. This accessibility follows from a full appreciation of what God has accomplished in Jesus' incarnation and the coming of the Holy Spirit. This shared life captures the essence of table fellowship that is prefigured in Abraham's table fellowship with three visitors in Genesis 18:1-15. This passage recounts an extraordinary encounter with God's messengers and perhaps even Godself. Abraham and Sarah hasten to prepare a meal for the three unexpected guests at the entrance to their tent. Like Abraham and Sarah, Christian teachers are called to put the feast on the table in their teaching. Anointed teaching is like artfully setting an inviting table that welcomes all to participate and can result in joyful celebration.[3] It can also result in lament with the

---

[3] Robert w. Pazmiño, *Basics of Teaching for Christians: Preparation, Instruction and Evaluation* (Grand Rapids: Baker Books, 1998), 11-12.

disclosure of shared suffering and despair. At table we consider with Abraham and Sarah "Is there anything too wonderful for the Lord?" At table the response of wonder and awe is nurtured.

Teachers rely upon God's Spirit graciously working both within and despite them sometimes in a paradoxical way.[4] Standing in the tradition of Jesus and following Jesus as his disciples, calls for honoring in faithful ways what Jesus modeled and taught. If Jesus can serve effectively as an exemplar that I have proposed in previous writings, Christian teachers must attend to those virtues that most cohere with his teaching practices. I identify five Christian virtues for teaching, namely love, faith, hope, joy and truth. In one setting where I taught on this topic, one participant, Roger White, helpfully proposed the additional virtue of humility to my lineup.[5] Being at table with Jesus and the Holy Spirit as a partner in teaching calls for humility when we sense the enormity of the task and the rich array of spiritual food offered.

## Humility

Humility can serve to identify how any virtues are embraced by Christians and how they are shared at table with others. Humility implies that if Christian teachers are actually incarnating Christ-like virtues these are communicated or taught to others in implicit rather than explicit ways. We are taught by how the table is set, how the food is prepared and how the guests are welcomed. Humility is the receptive stance of open hands and hearts that Christians maintain in relation to virtues that are spiritual gifts of God. Christians hold these virtues in the earthen or clay vessels of their human bodies (2 Cor 4:1-15, esp. v. 7). Christian teachers can celebrate the expression of Christian virtues incarnated in the life and ministry of Jesus, but not bring attention to themselves as paragons of virtue and worthy of emulation. Humility reminds Christian teachers of the ever present danger of arrogant self-righteousness in teaching. Humility can be explored in relation to pride. Table fellowship calls for table manners in recognizing the source of all gifts, spiritual and physical gifts. False pride is preoccupied with being better than others, whereas

---

[4] For a discussion of God's working in, through and despite Christian teachers see Robert W. Pazmiño, *God Our Teacher: Theological Basics in Christian Education* (Grand Rapids: Baker Academic, 2001), chapters 2, 4 and 5. Chapter 3 of that work explores the topic of God with us in the person and work of Jesus who serves as an exemplar for Christian teaching.

[5] Roger White of the Haggard School of Theology, Azusa Pacific University shared this insight at Talbot Theological Seminary, La Mirada, California on January 5, 2005 during a symposium I led on the theme of this book.

genuine pride considers one's gifts and works in relation to God's particular, personal and public call to teach.[6]

Genuine humility affirms the self as created by God and worthy, whereas false humility distorts that self either in an exaggerated or a diminished manner. Genuine pride and humility follow from Christians embracing their identity as children of God, disciples of Jesus and partners of the Holy Spirit in their teaching ministries. Paul suggested this in Romans 12:3: "For by the grace given to me I say to everyone among you not to think of yourself more highly than you ought to think, but to think with sober judgment, each according to the measure of faith that God has assigned." The complementary advice would be not to think of yourself lowlier than you ought to think. Genuine pride and humility lead to self-care and self-affirmation that does not deteriorate into self-hate or self-love that excludes God and others failing to obey Jesus' two great commandments of loving God and neighbor as ourselves.

Admission and confession are implied in identifying humility as a necessary stance in exploring Christian virtues. As Christians we admit our failings and confess our sins before a loving and forgiving God. This does not imply a quick rush to grace, but a sober assessment of what teachers hope others might imitate in our examples of living. As Christians we also admit our gifts and the fruits of our ministry as blessed by God.

The Book of Acts 2:42-47 describes the table fellowship that the followers of Jesus instituted in their times together following the birth of the Christian Church at Pentecost. The Holy Spirit launched the Christian Church and its ministries of teaching. Acts 2:42 notes: "They devoted themselves to the apostle's teaching and fellowship, to the breaking of bread and the prayers." The order of their activities is noteworthy. Teaching comes first followed by fellowship and the breaking of bread and prayers that suggests corporate worship and celebration. Identifying with Jesus and led by the Spirit results in faith practices following Jesus' departure from the earth and the sending of the Holy Spirit. Jesus' followers incarnate their faith and identify with him in their life together in table fellowship with the Holy Spirit.

Swiss theologian Karl Barth proposed that Christians participate in the three-fold work of the Holy Spirit. The threefold work included formation in tradition, communion of the saints, and the community of

---

[6] See a discussion of genuine and false pride in Robert W. Pazmiño, *By What Authority Do We Teach? Sources for Empowering Christian Educators* (Eugene, Ore.: Wipf and Stock, 2002), 74-75. John R. W. Scott has a helpful article "Am I supposed to love myself of hate myself? The cross points a way between self-love and self-denial," *Christianity Today* (April 20, 1984), 27-28.

witness.[7] This participation with the Holy Spirit extends the earthly ministry of Jesus upon his ascension and honors the manifestation of the Word of God initiated at creation with its ultimate fulfillment awaiting the consummation. This is a high calling for Christian teachers who recognize their reliance upon God's provision.

While recognizing Jesus' unique ministry and their own real limitations, Christian teachers also celebrate their identity as those graciously called by God to represent Jesus in their lives and ministries. This is a high calling that requires a daily and hourly reliance in prayer upon the resources made available to believers. The preeminent resource is the Spirit of Christ gifted to Jesus' followers upon his departure from the earth. The Spirit extends Jesus' ministry begun in the incarnation and waiting fulfillment at the second coming of Jesus to earth. The actual hope of Jesus' return serves as a motivation for holy living and faithful representation of those virtues Jesus honored in his journey and teaching ministry. (1 John 3:2-3) Part Two of this work considers the outworking of the table fellowship in relation to the celebration of the Christian virtues of truth, love, faith, hope and joy all held with a sense of humility by Christian teachers who seek to practice anointed teaching. The coming of the Holy Spirit at Pentecost makes possible anointed teaching sustained over time until the long-awaited consummation.

## Pentecostal Calling: Sustenance and Consummation

Teaching in the power of Jesus is often explored in the light of what occurred in Jesus' earthly journey after his crucifixion. As noted above in exploring the crucifixion from John 10:18b, Jesus is recorded as saying: "I have power to lay it (referring to his life) down, and I have power to take it up again." The crucifixion involved the laying down of his life and the resurrection involved his taking it up again. Power is manifested in each action, though most Christians associate power with the resurrection more than the crucifixion that can be associated with the power of both love and service. I find it noteworthy that Paul described the motto of his life in terms of both the crucifixion and resurrection in writing to the Christians he taught in Philippi: "I want to know Christ and the power of his resurrection and the sharing of his sufferings by becoming like him in his death, if somehow I may attain the resurrection from the dead." (Phil 3:10-11) Glimpses of both the crucifixion and resurrection are found in Jesus' teaching ministry prior to the historical events of Passion Week described vividly in the Gospels.

---

[7] Karl Barth, *Church Dogmatics* I, 1 (Edinburgh: T & T Clark, 1936), 88-124.

John 1:10-13 introduces the theme of transformation from this opening prologue to the gospel that describes Jesus' ministry on earth:

> He was in the world, and the world came into being through him; yet the world did not know him. He came to what was his own, and his own people did not accept him. But to all who received him, who believed in his name, he gave power to become children of God, who were born, not of blood or of the will of the flesh or of the will of man, but of God.

"Power to become the children of God" suggests a process of transformation that follows from believing in Jesus' name and receiving him as, for example, Nicodemus did over time and the Samarian woman in a shorter span of time. Power is experienced by having life in Jesus' name and in being born of God. Being born of God is the invitation that is both explicit and implicit in Jesus' teaching and extended to the teaching ministries of his disciples. These two persons encountered Jesus from different ends of the socioeconomic spectrum. A hunger exists for transformation at all levels of society and in all areas of human and created life. The dynamics may vary whether one is an outsider or insider of any particular human community.

To be treated as an outsider, as "the other" in any human encounter can deny one's personhood. Those viewed as the others are expendable. When survival is threatened, the other is most vulnerable. Martin Buber in his work *I and Thou* explores the importance of recognizing the personhood of all "others."[8] The openness to transformation can be radically different for outsiders as compared with insiders. Jesus transformed outsiders into insiders within his fellowship and on occasion insiders into outsiders in paradoxical ways. Jesus himself an outsider beyond his Galilean context could identify with those of outsider status in his first century world. For outsiders the longed for transformation may be viewed as an event compared with the process for insiders who have much to lose or relinquish in leaving the center and coming to the margins.

## Consummation

The table fellowship with Jesus at the Last Supper re-enacted at the celebration of the Lord's Supper, and the table fellowship with the Holy Spirit at Pentecost await their final fulfillment as described in Book of Revelation. The marriage supper of the lamb described in Revelation 19:1-10 is preceded by the angels singing the song of Moses and the song

---

[8] Marin Buber, *I and Thou* (New York: Charles Scribner's Sons, 1970).

of the Lamb. The Song of Moses from Deuteronomy 32 is also mentioned in Revelation 15:3-4. As K. H. Bartels notes "the other song of Moses in the Old Testament is found in Exodus 15:1-18 where Moses and the Israelites celebrated the deliverance from Pharaoh's army and the liberation of the people. The writer of Revelation, John, transposes the song of Moses in Exodus 15 and also includes words from Psalm 145:7 giving them Christological significance."[9] Psalm 145 celebrates the greatness and goodness of God and verse 7 reads: "They shall celebrate the fame of your abundant goodness, and shall sing aloud of your righteousness."

Returning to Revelation 15: 3, we read: "And they (referring to the seven angels) sing the song of Moses, the servant of God, and the song of the Lamb:

Here is the "Song of the Lamb:"
Great and amazing are your deeds, Lord God the Almighty!
Just and true are your ways, King of the nations!
Lord, who will not fear and glorify your name?
For you alone are holy.
All nations will come and worship before you,
for your judgments have been revealed.

This glorious Song of the Lamb celebrates what the Second Moses, our Lord Jesus Christ accomplished and all we need to communicate through our teaching ministries to a world with great spiritual need and hunger awaiting the establishment of a New Heaven and New Earth (Revelation 21) fulfilling God's purposes for all of creation with a new creation made possible through the ministries of Jesus Christ and the Holy Spirit working in partnership with God the Father. Father, Son and Spirit model for humanity the anointed partnership necessary to accomplish God's purposes in a renewed earth.

In returning to Deuteronomy 32:5-14 we discover that all is not well with the generations and the Lord's people personified in the person of Jacob and his descendants. But despite it all and despite us, God sustains and cares for those people seeking to follow God's ways. God's care and grace 'despite us' is a message of hope amid God's judgment. God sustains us in our learning and in our teaching throughout our lives.

Teaching can be inherently a hopeful venture for it assumes and proposes that some folk are gathered together and capable of learning. It also suggests that the teachers or teachers have something of value to share. In the case of Christian faith, teaching affirms the belief that God

---

[9] Bartels, 674

is our Teacher. God was the teacher of Abraham, Isaac and Jacob; and God was the teacher of Sarah, Rebekah, Leah and Rachel. God has been the teacher of our lives from the very knitting of our bodies in our mother's womb as beautifully described in Psalm 139:13-16, from our passing through birth into this world, and from the journeys of our lives to this very point today. Do we sense and appreciate the wonder of that gift of God's sustaining presence and teaching in all of life? What hope can we bring to our lives and the lives of others in a time of global economic crisis or recession and national challenge?

Teaching that sustains us involves both denunciation and annunciation. With the denunciation of the destroyers of life comes the possibility of announcing the new life God is bringing into our lives. The New Testament pattern is life, death and new life in Jesus Christ and the coming of the Holy Spirit. Gabriel Moran in his work *Showing How: The Act of Teaching* suggests that to teach is to show how to live and how to die.[10] I would add to teach is to show how to love and to live again, to live anew through God's gracious transformation and renewal gifted to us by God's Spirit, the Spirit of Jesus, the Blessed Holy Spirit who anoints our teaching ministries. Anointed teaching sustains persons, communities, societies and all of creation that is hankering and groaning for new life (Romans 8:18-30). All of Jesus' disciples turned their first century world upside down, so we are invited to do the same today. Anointed teaching fosters the love of God, neighbor, self and all of creation.

## Conclusion

The search for a practical pneumatology celebrates the theological basics of the Spirit's liberation, celebration, and sustenance as essentials for Christian teaching. As Steve Kang notes in describing truth-embodying communities, Christian communities are ones in which "the life, death and resurrection of Jesus Christ are celebrated and continue to shape the way of life of its people through the power of the Holy Spirit,"[11] Christian teachers support the spiritual formation and growth of such communities as they consider with their students what is required of us in our partnership with the Holy Spirit. The power and partnership with the Spirit undergirds anointed teaching in the world and provides

---

[10] Gabriel Morán, p. 39
[11] S. Steve Kang, "Truth-Embodying Households," in *Growing Healthy Asian American Churches*, edited by Peter Cha, S. Steve Kang and Helen Lee (Downers Grove, Ill.: InterVarsity Press, 2006), 48.

insights for the thoughts and practices of Christian teachers across the ages.

PART ONE

# Teaching in the Spirit and Liberation

Having explored theological basics for a practical pneumatology, one question lingers: Anointed teaching, what is it? In the New Testament, according to the scholar Dietrich Müller, anointing "is a *metaphor* for the bestowal of the Holy Spirit, special power, or a divine commission."[12] (Müller, 122) James Wilhoit and Linda Rozema in their article "Anointed Teaching" distinguish the Spirit within, upon and among those who teach in their ministries.[13] We prefer to consider here the fruits of anointed teaching, namely the fruits of liberation leading to justice, celebration, and sustenance suggested from consideration of the Song of Moses and Mary's Magnificat. In our writings we refer to the Blessed Holy Spirit, third person of the Trinity, endowing, empowering, and enabling Christians to be transformed into the image of Jesus Christ through their faithful reliance upon God and the Living Christ in their teaching ministries. The gift of teaching is a spiritual gift that God bestows upon God's people to pass on a living and vital faith in a desperate world in need of good news. The Spirit is poured upon the disciples of Jesus to fulfill the educational commission of Matthew 28:18-20, the commission of making disciples in all the world, baptizing them in the name of the Father, Son and Spirit, and teaching them to obey all that Jesus himself taught. Whereas the earlier work *God Our Teacher* explored teaching in the name of our Creator God, and *So What Makes Our Teaching Christian?* explored teaching in the name of Jesus the Son, this work explores the person and ministry of the Holy Spirit, third person of the Trinity. The challenge of teaching other persons to obey all that Jesus taught far transcends our usual associations with teaching and requires the essential ministry of the Holy Spirit to work within us, within other persons, within the faith community, the wider local community, the

---

[12] Müller, 122
[13] Wilhoit and Rozema, 245

nations of the globe, and all of creation that groans in anticipation of God's full and complete salvation (Rom 8:18-27).

Deuteronomy 32 has intrigued us because the beginning verses of Moses' song described anointed teaching for which humanity longs:

Listen, O heavens and I will speak;
Hear, O earth, the words of my mouth.
Let my teaching fall like rain
And my words descend like dew,
Like showers on new grass,
Like abundant rain on tender plants.
I will proclaim the name of the Lord.
Oh, praise the greatness of our God!
He is the Rock, his words are perfect,
And all his ways are just.
A faithful God who does no wrong,
Upright and just is he.

As noted in Deut. 31:19, this song, which was a song of witness to God's covenant people, was taught in order that they themselves might sing it. Moses' song was taught on an occasion when he recounted his leadership and ministry, and viewed the potential of the Promised Land for the people of God. The song includes practical advice to remind and educate the people in the way they should go. Moses encouraged his fellow travelers to choose life as offered by their caring and liberating God.

Moses spoke about an education that liberates. His teaching was to bring life and refreshment to those coming from a desert experience. In Kathleen Norris' book *The Cloister Walk,* it is noted that Mechtild of Magdeburg, a medieval mystic suggested that we see ourselves as dusty desert acres in need of the life-giving rain of Christ and the gentle dew of the Holy Spirit in our lives and our teaching.[14] Teaching is to flow from our lives lived in close communion with the Triune God made possible today through the ministry of the Holy Spirit. What rain meant to those who wandered in the wilderness, and to plant life there, so the challenge today for our teaching that it should issue forth as refreshment, bringing forth life and growth. Our teaching as Christians, if anointed by God's Spirit, is to issue in life, liberating seeds and growth long held dormant in human hearts and fulfilling all God intended from the beginnings of creation. In the realm of human life, growth is toward God's *shalom* that embodies peace and justice for all.

---

[14] Kathleen Norris, *The Cloister Walk* (New York: Riverhead Books, 1996), 159.

Moses' song had potential for the lives of the covenant people. If his teaching penetrated and saturated their hearts and minds, then it would enable them to grow in their relationship to their Lord. The reason the words of the song had such a potential was because of its subject matter, which was God. The people's relationship with God was the essential concern and focus of this teaching and that which enabled liberation. Liberation can be defined as freedom for life as God intended. As we move to the New Testament, liberation is realized through the saving work of Jesus Christ (a second Moses), which is pictured for us as inviting a new exodus and new life gifted by the Spirit of Jesus the Christ following the endowment gifted to Jesus' followers at Pentecost with the birthing the Christian church.

The Apostle Paul describes the liberation made possible for Jesus' followers through life in the Spirit:

> So then, brothers and sisters, we are debtors, not to the flesh, to live according to the flesh—for if you live according to the flesh, you will die; but if by the Spirit you put to death the deeds of the body, you will live. For all who are led by the Spirit of God are children of God. For you did not receive a spirit of slavery to fall back into fear, but you received a spirit of adoption. When we cry, "Abba! Father!" it is that very Spirit bearing witness with our spirit that we are children of God, and if children, then heirs, heirs of God and joint heirs with Christ—if, in fact, we suffer with him so that we may also be glorified with him. (Romans 8: 12-17)

The spirit of slavery and fear is replaced with the spirit of adoption and liberation that embraces our full rights as heirs of God and joint heirs with Christ as was intended from creation. The Spirit that originally breathed into the dust to bring forth life now breathes new life into God's adopted children witnessing to human spirits their renewed and free status, free to serve God and neighbor with all the gifts God bestows on believers.

Moses' song finds clear echoes in Hannah's prayer and song recorded in 1 Samuel 2:1-10 where she honors God's gift and dedicates her son to God's service as will also later be the case for Mary's Song known as the Magnificat recorded in Luke's Gospel:

> Hannah prayed and said,
> "My heart exults in the LORD;
> my strength is exalted in my God.
> My mouth derides my enemies,
> because I rejoice in my victory.

"There is no Holy One like the LORD,
no one besides you;
there is no Rock like our God.
Talk no more so very proudly,
let not arrogance come from your mouth;
for the LORD is a God of knowledge,
and by him actions are weighed.
The bows of the mighty are broken,
but the feeble gird on strength.
Those who were full have hired themselves out for bread,
but those who were hungry are fat with spoil.
The barren has borne seven,
but she who has many children is forlorn.
The LORD kills and brings to life;
he brings down to Sheol and raises up.
The LORD makes poor and makes rich;
he brings low, he also exalts.
He raises up the poor from the dust;
he lifts the needy from the ash heap,
to make them sit with princes
and inherit a seat of honor.
For the pillars of the earth are the LORD's,
and on them he has set the world.
"He will guard the feet of his faithful ones,
but the wicked shall be cut off in darkness;
for not by might does one prevail.
The LORD! His adversaries shall be shattered;
the Most High will thunder in heaven.
The LORD will judge the ends of the earth;
he will give strength to his king,
and exalt the power of his anointed."

Hannah experiences liberation from her childless alienation with the birth of a son and she reflects on God's intentions for all of creation bearing the fruits of liberation, celebration, and sustenance for humankind and all creation. God's anointed ones create new possibilities for life working in partnership with God.

Hannah's song is a prelude to what Mary, Jesus' mother shares with her cousin Elizabeth as they share the joy of bearing children, the fruit of their wombs. Mary's Song is significant if we recall that she was Jesus' first teacher as his mother. Mary's Song is known as the Magnificat for it begins with her magnifying the Lord God for God's blessings in giving new life:

And Mary said,
"My soul magnifies the Lord,
and my spirit rejoices in God my Savior,
for he has looked with favor on the lowliness of his servant.
Surely, from now on all generations will call me blessed;
for the Mighty One has done great things for me,
and holy is his name.
His mercy is for those who fear him
from generation to generation. He has shown strength with his arm;
he has scattered the proud in the thoughts of their hearts.
He has brought down the powerful from their thrones,
and lifted up the lowly;
he has filled the hungry with good things,
and sent the rich away empty.
He has helped his servant Israel,
in remembrance of his mercy,
according to the promise he made to our ancestors,
to Abraham and to his descendants forever."

The theme of celebration in terms of praise is paramount for Mary as was the case for Hannah, yet the themes of both liberation and justice in God's actions on behalf of the humble, the lowly and the hungry and the sustenance of good things and strength shared with the weak are also worthy of singing and resound in both Mary's and Hannah's voices alike. The fruit of their wombs blesses them personally and all of humanity in God's provision for humankind.

For Christians today, an education that liberates has implications for the *personal* as well as the *social* dimensions of our lives. First, in the personal dimension, in the realm of our inner life and that of our students, education that liberates has implications for our experience of redemption and personal piety or holiness, known today as spirituality. As teachers of the Christian faith, we are called to use our power to free and empower others, to share the essential content of our faith, and to seek to understand the implications of the Abba-ship of God and Lordship of Christ for all areas of our personal life. The focus of such teaching is to be *doing* the will of God, and not just knowing God's will. The truth of God in Jesus Christ is to be lived through the power of the indwelling Holy Spirit in our lives and in the lives of our students. For this to occur, we as Christian educators are called to share our lives as well as our teachings with our students. As Galatians 5:25 teaches: "If we live by the Spirit, let us also be guided by the Spirit." We would add, let us be guided by the Spirit in our teaching and learning together in community towards God's ends for all of creation.

Lest we become limited to the *personal* dimension, we come to realize that authentic Christian spirituality is both personal and *social* or *corporate* in nature. When our relationship to God in our personal lives is overemphasized to the exclusion of the larger social world, it can easily become selfish, self-absorbed, and sinful, "according to the flesh" in Paul's description. This is a limited spirituality and holiness that centers solely upon us. Thus, education that liberates must secondly deal with the full social dimensions of life.

In our educational efforts, we are called to grapple with understanding how God's revelation impacts upon our society and our diverse cultures. Through education, we must confront the implications of the Lordship of Christ for all areas of social interaction, including the political, social, cultural and economic spheres. Spiritual discernment is crucial in our public lives. For we who live in an institutionalized society, such implications include those for institutional life, for how we treat other persons and how we accomplish tasks. In our current situation, we must also wrestle with God's concern for the poor and oppressed, and the plights of urban, suburban and rural areas, both nationally and globally with spiritual discernment and imagination.

But, as with the personal dimension, there needs to be caution in this social dimension. This is the case because sometimes we can overemphasize our relationship to the world and others at the expense of our relationship to God and to our inner spiritual life. When this happens, worldly and social concerns become shallow, empty, and foundationless. Thus, there needs to be a fresh and exciting dialogue and interaction between the personal and social dimensions of our faith in an education that liberates. For a public pneumatology it is necessary to balance personal and social life, individuality and connectivity, private life and public life. The pressing need is to think of the common weal, the commonwealth, and the common and public good in Christian teaching.[15] This was brought home to Bob in an experience he had in 2006.

Back on June 13, 2006 Bob and his wife Wanda were invited to attend the festive Boston Pops Orchestra by their Jewish friends Heni and Mark whose daughter Sarah Koenig-Plonskier was playing as the Winner of the Boston Orchestra Concerto Competition. Also on the program that night was the presentation of "The Four Freedoms" symphony by Robert Russell Bennett that captured Bob's spiritual imagination. That

---

[15] See the insights of Benjamin Valentin, *Mapping Public Theology: Beyond Culture, Identity, and Difference* (Harrisburg, Pa.: Trinity Press International, 2002), 94.

symphony was inspired and named after the four paintings of Norman Rockwell completed in 1943.

The four beloved freedoms originally were named by President Franklin D. Roosevelt (FDR) on January 6, 1941 when he addressed Congress and delivered his historic "Four Freedoms" speech. FDR's speech so inspired the painter and illustrator Norman Rockwell that he created a series of paintings on the "Four Freedoms" theme. Rockwell interpreted the four freedoms in terms of everyday life. The paintings served as the centerpiece of a national war bonds drive that rose over $130 million and helped to publicly teach folk regarding the aims of U.S. involvement in World War II.[16]

What were the four freedoms that so inspired artists and composers along with a host of ordinary persons in a time of national and international crisis and struggle? First, freedom of speech and expression valued the voice and agency of all people everywhere in the world. Second, freedom of worship valued human spirits in their religious expression hopefully activated by God's Spirit to offer reverence and praise, wonder and awe before the Creator. Third, freedom from want in everyday life affirmed the basic human needs of food, clothing, shelter, medical care and educational opportunity and raises the question of human rights amid various forms of oppression encountered in the world. Fourth, freedom from fear given the human propensity for violence, abuse, greed, and privilege challenges the principalities and powers of the world system which stand in stark contrast with God's vision for peace with justice throughout creation. These four freedoms serve to guide our discussion of anointed teaching that liberates; our anointed teaching that bears the fruit of liberation.

Jesus himself in his teaching ministry as described in Luke's Gospel, chapter four, models the connection between his anointed teaching and the fruit of liberation promised to his hearers following his baptism in Luke 3: 21-22 and his forty-day temptation (4:1-13) that identifies opposition and challenges for what Jesus proposes to initiate in his reign:

> Now when all the people were baptized, and when Jesus also had been baptized and was praying, the heaven was opened, and the Holy Spirit descended upon him in bodily form like a dove. And a voice came from heaven, "You are my Son, the Beloved; with you I am well pleased."

---

[16] For an updated portrayal of the four freedoms, see "Revisiting Rockwell" by Abigail Tucker and photographs by Jason Pietra that was published in the March 2018 periodical "Smithsonian" pp. 7-14 that honors contemporary artists' contributions to representing the enduring virtues captured in the four freedoms.

Jesus, full of the Holy Spirit, returned from the Jordan and was led by the Spirit in the wilderness, where for forty days he was tempted by the devil. He ate nothing at all during those days, and when they were over, he was famished. The devil said to him, "If you are the Son of God, command this stone to become a loaf of bread." Jesus answered him, "It is written, 'One does not live by bread alone.'" Then the devil led him up and showed him in an instant all the kingdoms of the world. And the devil said to him, "To you I will give their glory and all this authority; for it has been given over to me, and I give it to anyone I please. If you, then, will worship me, it will all be yours." Jesus answered him, "It is written, 'Worship the Lord your God, and serve only him.'" Then the devil took him to Jerusalem, and placed him on the pinnacle of the temple, saying to him, "If you are the Son of God, throw yourself down from here, for it is written, 'He will command his angels concerning you, to protect you,' and 'On their hands they will bear you up, so that you will not dash your foot against a stone.'" Jesus answered him, "It is said, 'Do not put the Lord your God to the test.'" When the devil had finished every test, he departed from him until an opportune time. Then Jesus, filled with the power of the Spirit, returned to Galilee, and a report about him spread through all the surrounding country. He began to teach in their synagogues and was praised by everyone. When he came to Nazareth, where he had been brought up, he went to the synagogue on the sabbath day, as was his custom. He stood up to read, and the scroll of the prophet Isaiah was given to him. He unrolled the scroll and found the place where it was written: "The Spirit of the Lord is upon me, because he has anointed me to bring good news to the poor. He has sent me to proclaim release to the captives and recovery of sight to the blind, to let the oppressed go free, to proclaim the year of the Lord's favor." And he rolled up the scroll, gave it back to the attendant, and sat down. The eyes of all in the synagogue were fixed on him. Then he began to say to them, "Today this scripture has been fulfilled in your hearing." All spoke well of him and were amazed at the gracious words that came from his mouth. They said, "Is not this Joseph's son?" He said to them, "Doubtless you will quote to me this proverb, 'Doctor, cure yourself!'" And you will say, "Do here also in your hometown the things that we have heard you did at Capernaum." And he said, "Truly I tell you, no prophet is accepted in the prophet's hometown. But the truth is, there were many widows in Israel in the time of Elijah, when the heaven was shut up three years and six months, and there was a severe famine over all the land; yet Elijah was sent to none of them except to a widow at Zarephath in Sidon. There were also many lepers in Israel in the time of the prophet Elisha, and none of them was cleansed except Naaman the Syrian." When they heard this, all in the synagogue were filled with rage. They got up, drove him out of the town, and led him to the brow of the hill on which their town was built, so that they might hurl him off the cliff. But he passed through the midst of them and went on his way.

Following his baptism where the Holy Spirit descended upon him, Jesus was full of the Spirit and led by the Spirit into the wilderness where he was severely tested, but sustained by the Spirit and God's Word through various temptations that still plague humanity. Then filled with the power of the Spirit, he returned to Galilee and began to teach. In his initial public teaching, he made explicit the Spirit's anointing him to bring good news of liberation from all forms of oppression clearly noted in Luke's text that draws upon Isaiah's prophetic vision (Isa 61:1-2; 58:6-7) and the good news of God's deliverance for the people. Jesus, as a Spirit-filled prophetic teacher, celebrated the fruit of liberation in his public teaching. Those who follow Jesus in their teaching are called to a similar ministry bearing the fruit of liberation in its various forms.

The task of liberation can be seen in relation to three distinct levels insightfully identified by Gustavo Gutierrez which, though distinct, are intimately connected in everyday life. The first level of liberation is socioeconomic and political, seeking the empowerment and release of the oppressed, the exploited classes, despised ethnic groups, and folk from marginalized cultures, who must receive full access to resources they need to live. This level represents the aspirations of all oppressed people. In relation to this level, the church is called to a ministry of advocacy for and identification with those who are voiceless and powerless under current social arrangements and privilege. The second level of liberation represents a distinct understanding of history, in which persons assume conscious responsibility for their destinies. Cooperation, partnership, and the worth of each person's life are the values affirmed at this level. Each individual is viewed as having dignity and worth, deserving care and concern, throughout life and even in death. In relation to this level, the church is called upon to model a community of care and concern for all persons. The third level of liberation is theological and spiritual, calling for the liberation from sin, which is viewed as the ultimate root of all injustice and oppression. This third level includes communion with God and God's people. All three levels of liberation are seen by Gutierrez as part of God's one salvific process and worthy of consideration by Christians.[17] This theological and spiritual liberation enables people to fully embrace a life of community in partnership with the Holy Spirit and participation in fulfilling God's mission in the world. It recognizes that persons both sin and have been sinned against by

---

[17] Gustavo Gutiérrez, *A Theology of Liberation: History, Politics and Salvation*, trans. Sister Caridad Inda and John Eagleson (Maryknoll, N. Y.: Orbis, 1973), 36-37, 176.

societal systems and structures that perpetuate oppression and squelch liberation in systematic ways that call for works of justice.

Hispanic Christian ethicist Eldin Villafañe provides helpful insights for how God's Spirit as the Liberating Spirit invites our full participation in his ministry in our faith practices like teaching. He presents a paradigm that links our theological self-understanding of the Spirit to an ethical self-understanding that has implications for anointed teaching. The paradigm is threefold and emerges from Galatians 5:25 where Paul reminds believers that both our theological self-understanding and our ethical self-understanding are grounded in the Spirit: "If we live in the Spirit (theological), let us also be guided by the Spirit (ethical)." The threefold paradigm named by Villafañe includes the following:

1. The Spirit's historical project-the challenge to participate in the reign of God.
2. The Spirit's power encounters-the challenge to confront structural sin and evil.
3. The Spirit's charismatic empowerment-the challenge to fulfill the prophetic and vocational role of the baptism in the Spirit.[18]

There is a noteworthy parallel between the insights of Villafañe and Gutierrez for grasping the extent of the Holy Spirit's ministry in the full liberation of humanity and all of creation. Through the Spirit's ministry of baptizing and anointing followers of Jesus, the liberation Jesus proclaimed finds expression at all levels of personal, communal and corporate life while Christians contend with opposition and challenges similar to those Jesus himself encountered in his earthly ministry as noted in Luke's account.

A statement from *The Lausanne Covenant* written in 1975 serves to affirm what this introduction to Part One suggests is one of the first fruits of anointed teaching:

CHRISTIAN SOCIAL RESPONSIBILITY

We affirm that God is both the Creator and the Judge of all people. We therefore should share his concern for justice and reconciliation throughout human society and for the liberation of men and women from every kind of oppression. Because men and women are made in the image of God, every person, regardless of race, religion, color, culture, class, sex or age, has an intrinsic dignity because of which he or she should be respected and served, not exploited. Here too we express

---

[18] Eldin Villafañe, *The Liberating Spirit: Toward an Hispanic American Pentecostal Social Ethic* (Grand Rapids: Eerdmans, 1993), 194-195.

penitence both for our neglect and for having sometimes regarded evangelism and social concern as mutually exclusive. Although reconciliation with other people is not reconciliation with God, nor is social action evangelism, nor is political liberation salvation, nevertheless we affirm that evangelism and socio-political involvement are both part of our Christian duty. For both are necessary expressions of our doctrines of God and man, our love for our neighbor and our obedience to Jesus Christ. The message of salvation implies also a message of judgment upon every form of alienation, oppression and discrimination, and we should not be afraid to denounce evil and injustice wherever they exist. When people receive Christ they are born again into his kingdom and must seek not only to exhibit but also to spread its righteousness in the midst of an unrighteous world. The salvation we claim should be transforming us in the totality of our personal and social responsibilities. Faith without works is dead. (Acts 17:26, 31; Gen. 18:25; Isa. 1:17; Psa. 45:7; Gen. 1:26, 27; Jas. 3:9; Lev. 19:18; Luke 6:27, 35; Jas. 2:14-26; John 3:3, 5; Matt. 5:20; 6:33; 2 Cor. 3:18; Jas. 2:20)[19]

John Perkins who has devoted his life to Christian social ministry with those on the margins shares his words that are as timely as when originally penned: "God's will is plain. We are to love Him and love people. The Biblical evidence overwhelmingly states that the will of God is to love Him in a way that leaves no room for idols and to love our neighbor in a way that liberates him from poverty and oppression either spiritual or physical."[20] One of the first fruits of anointed teaching is liberation with which the Spirit seeks to bless us. Moses, Hannah and Mary in their songs make that clear as they teach others what they have learned. Jesus also taught the same in his two great commandments that include love of God and our neighbor (Luke 10:27). Jesus also exemplified this love as a high priest in the giving of his life through the eternal or Holy Spirit: "how much more will the blood of Christ, who through the eternal Spirit offered himself without blemish to God, purify our conscience from dead works to worship the living God!" (Hebrews 9:14) The living God in the person of Jesus and the power of the Spirit offers liberation or true freedom to humankind and all of creation for which many long throughout human history.

---

[19] John Stott, *The Lausanne Covenant: An Exposition and Commentary* (Minneapolis: World Wide Publications, 1975), 25.
[20] John Perkins, *A Quiet Revolution* (Waco, Tex.: Word Books, 1976), 33-34.

CHAPTER 2

# Teaching and Freedom of Speech and Expression
Octavio J. Esqueda

I once called a friend to catch up and when I asked him if he had time to talk he answered positively because he was just reading the news in the local newspaper. I then asked him if he had found an article with good news and he quickly replied with a firm "no." We all can relate to him because it seems that we only receive bad news and for some reason the good news usually go unnoticed. For this reason, it sadly easy for us to focus primarily on the negative situations around us and forget the positive ones.

Nevertheless, we do need to acknowledge that we are living in difficult times. Unfortunately, we live in a world affected by sin where injustice, racism, and inequality are common elements in our society and we all can see their effects in our surroundings. In these circumstances and in the middle of a polarized environment, the easiest approach to take is to remain silent and to avoid get involved in controversial issues. In fact, for many believers and Christian educators this attitude is prevalent and they argue that their focus primarily centers on "spiritual" issues and intentionally set aside any "social" or "mundane" issues. The truth is, however, that a healthy theology (orthodoxy) without a healthy practice (orthopraxis) not only is incomplete, but in fact it becomes sinful as James 4:17 reminds us, "Therefore, to one who knows *the* right thing to do and does not do it, to him it is sin." The Christian faith and the ministry of the Holy Spirit must have influence in all areas of our society and they break the false dichotomy between what is considered sacred and mundane because the Lordship of Christ rules over everything in this world and in our lives.

Consequently, a Christian under the anointing and guide of the Holy Spirit should proclaim the message of redemption in Christ to all people and to all life circumstances regardless of how difficult they might be. The Holy Spirit message is prophetic in the middle of the most difficult conditions. Also, all believers enjoy the freedom of thought and spiritual

37

expression that the Holy Spirit bestows to them. Followers of Christ have been set free from human legalism that attempts to earn God's favor with human merits. For this reason, Christ offers true freedom of speech and expression on behalf of others and ourselves in order to grow in his knowledge and his grace (John 8:36; 2 Peter 3:18).

## Freedom of Speech and Expression on Behalf of Others

Christian teaching cannot remain silent in the present difficulties around us. In fact, silence demonstrates a clear position of indifference for the needs of other people. The reverend Martin Luther King Jr. rightly pointed out in his famous *Letter from Birmingham Jail* the following: "We will have to repent in this generation not merely for the hateful words and actions of the bad people but for the appalling silence of the good people."[21] Believers cannot remain silent or remain on the sidelines against injustices. We cannot remain neutral when some people are facing oppression as Desmont Totu reminds us, "If you are neutral in situations of injustice, you have chosen the side of the oppressor."[22]

Therefore, as Christian educators we are called to use our liberty of expression to defend and support those who are marginalized. Obviously, our task is to remain faithful to the Lord and to teach the Word of God. When we do it, we honor what God honors and we value what God values. Teaching with the Spirit's leading always desires the edification and wellbeing of others. Bernard of Clairvaux rightly clarifies the difference that our knowledge and teaching makes when we focus on others, "Some seek knowledge for the sake of knowledge: this is curiosity; others seek knowledge so that they themselves may be known: that is vanity; but there are still others who seek knowledge in order to serve and edify others: and that is charity."[23]

As Christian leaders we need to speak on behalf of those who are oppressed and to seek that people listen to their voices. For example, lately in the United States hundreds of stories regarding sexual abuse and discrimination have circulated in social media. Many actors, communicators, leaders and politicians have been accused of abusing and sometimes sexually assaulting other people, mainly women, with complete impunity. Until now, because these public accusations in several instances have forced that many perpetrators finally face labor or

---

[21] Martin Luther King Jr. "Letter from the Birmingham jail." In *Why We Can't Wait*, ed. Martin Luther King, Jr.,

[22] Desmont Tutu As quoted in *Unexpected News: Reading the Bible with Third World Eyes* (1984) by Robert McAfee Brown, 19

[23] Lewis A. Drummond. *El Amor: Lo más grande del mundo.* (Grand Rapids, MI: Portavoz, 2004), 23

criminal consequences. At last, the voices of the victims are being heard after years of painful silence.

For everyone in our society, but especially for followers of Christ is extremely important that we acknowledge the voices of those who long for justice, equality, and dignity. The Bible teaches that all men and women are created in the image of God and that all people have intrinsic value and dignity (Gen. 1:27). God is the one who created our sexuality and designed to be expressed in a context of intimacy, respect, and love. Therefore, any activity that diminishes the value and dignity of any human being must be rejected and punished.

Abuse of power is the common denominator for the stories of sexual abuse and assault that continue emerging around us. Abusers, primarily men, had authority and power over their victims. Unfortunately, they abused their power to intimidate and abuse others and even forbid them to share their experiences. This situation continues to this day in all areas of our society, including churches and religious institutions. For this reason, it becomes imperative that we all revise the power structures in our organizations and that we try to be more inclusive to all. We need the active participation of all in the decision-making process and in the leadership structures. In addition, listening to the voices of those who courageously share their abuse stories and believing them are essential tasks for all of us. The actress Salma Hayek told for the first time her story of abuse from the movie producer Harvey Weinstein in a New York Times article. In this piece Hayek shares the reason why many have abuse others and why we are only hearing their stories until now. Her words reminds us the importance of listening and advocating for other people and to work together to finally put an end to these kind of stories:

> I am grateful for everyone who is listening to our experiences. I hope that adding my voice to the chorus of those who are finally speaking out will shed light on why it is so difficult, and why so many of us have waited so long. Men sexually harassed because they could. Women are talking today because, in this new era, we finally can.[24]

Therefore, a very important duty as Christian educators is to proclaim the liberating message of God to those who struggle with any kind of oppression or face difficult circumstances. Biblical teaching is prophetic when we speak God's message. In this way, the terms "prophecy" and

---

[24] Salma Hayek. *Harvey Weinstein is my Monster Too.* The New York Times Opinion, December 12, 2017 (https://www.nytimes.com/es/2017/12/13/salma-hayek-harvey-weinstein/).

"preaching" to some extent go together.[25] The prophetic voice of Christian teaching brings hope, consolation, and renewal in a world corrupted by sin. We should use our freedom in Christ to proclaim the good news of God's kingdom so everybody can receive God's direction and receive divine consolation.

However, it is essential that the Holy Spirit directs our words. The message with the Holy Spirit's anointing always concurs with the Scriptures. The same Spirit who inspired the biblical authors is the one who uses us to proclaim the good news of Christ that brings light to a desperate world:

> *So* we have the prophetic word *made* more sure, to which you do well to pay attention as to a lamp shining in a dark place, until the day dawns and the morning star arises in your hearts. But know this first of all, that no prophecy of Scripture is *a matter* of one's own interpretation, for no prophecy was ever made by an act of human will, but men moved by the Holy Spirit spoke from God (2 Peter 1:19-21).

In the Gospel of Luke, we have two clear examples about how the Holy Spirit's anointing directs our words and actions. Anointed teaching becomes powerful with the Holy Spirit. Luke 1:67-79 tells Zachariah's prophecy when his son John, we later would become John the Baptist, was presented at the temple. Zachariah's prophetic words express the divine blessing for the coming birth of the Messiah, for the ministry that his son will have and because God's grace reaches all human beings. This prayer is also a model that shows how the Holy Spirit's leading always directs us to a life of obedience and holiness.

> *And his father Zacharias was filled with the Holy Spirit,* and prophesied, saying:
> "Blessed *be* the Lord God of Israel,
> For He has visited us and accomplished redemption for His people,
> And has raised up a horn of salvation for us
> In the house of David His servant—
> As He spoke by the mouth of His holy prophets from of old—
> Salvation FROM OUR ENEMIES,
> And FROM THE HAND OF ALL WHO HATE US;
> To show mercy toward our fathers,
> And to remember His holy covenant,
> The oath which He swore to Abraham our father,
> To grant us that we, being rescued from the hand of our enemies,

---

[25] Gonzalez, Justo L., "Prophecy," en *Essential Theological Terms* (Louisville, KY: Westminster John Knox Press, 2005), 142.

*Might serve Him* without fear,
*In holiness and righteousness before Him all our days.*
"And you, child, will be called the prophet of the Most High;
For you will go on BEFORE THE LORD TO PREPARE HIS WAYS;
To give to His people *the knowledge* of salvation
By the forgiveness of their sins,
Because of the tender mercy of our God,
With which the Sunrise from on high will visit us,
TO SHINE UPON THOSE WHO SIT IN DARKNESS AND THE SHADOW OF
DEATH,
*To guide our feet into the way of peace.*" (emphasis mine)

This hymn known as the *Benedictus* (for the first word in the Latin translation) is "a great general vision about the fulfillment of God's promise of salvation and liberation" where now "the hope of the saints is their rescue and redemption that equips them to a consecrated service to God."[26] The anointing of the Spirit produces holiness and a desire to walk in a path of divine justice and peace. Through the Holy Spirit we receive the freedom to proclaim God's goodness on behalf of others in spite of the present difficulties.

Simeon and Anna were two pious people who had the great privilege to see and bless the baby Jesus when he was presented at the temple. Luke 2:25-38 tells the story of how Simeon, a righteous and devout man, and Anna, a prophetess advanced in years, were able to see the Messiah they expected all of their lives. Both of them were the first one who publicly declared that Jesus was the Christ that would bring redemption to the whole world. The Holy Spirit guided their words and actions. Luke makes clear that the Holy Spirit was upon Simeon (Luke 2:25), and, consequently, The Holy Spirit guided his words.

> *And it had been revealed to him by the Holy Spirit* that he would not see death before he had seen the Lord's Christ. And he came *in the Spirit* into the temple; and when the parents brought in the child Jesus, to carry out for Him the custom of the Law, then he took Him into his arms, *and blessed God, and said,*
> "Now Lord, You are releasing Your bond-servant to depart in peace, According to Your word;
> For my eyes have seen Your salvation,
> Which You have prepared in the presence of all peoples,
> A LIGHT OF REVELATION TO THE GENTILES,
> And the glory of Your people Israel" (Luke 2:26-32, emphasis mine).

---

[26] Darrell L. Bock. *Comentario Bíblico con Aplicación NVI: Lucas* (Miami, FL: Editorial Vida, 2011), 71

Simeon demonstrates to us how the Holy Spirit's anointing leads us to proclaim the Lord's liberating message to a needy world. Anointed teaching always produces the fruits of freedom of speech and expression on behalf of others. The prophetic voice of those who have placed Christ at the center of their lives becomes a balsam of hope to the audience.

Our Lord Jesus Christ during his earthly ministry also illustrates to us how the Holy Spirit's anointing was the source of his words and that his message brought hope to those who were oppressed. Luke 4:14-15 describes the beginning of Jesus public ministry where his teaching and the Holy Spirit's power always were together, "And Jesus returned to Galilee *in the power of the Spirit,* and news about Him spread through all the surrounding district. And He *began* teaching in their synagogues and was praised by all." Therefore, Jesus proclaimed with complete clarity that his calling was to announce to everybody the good news of the kingdom of God. Luke continues the story with Jesus proclamation of his messianic ministry in Nazareth, the town where he grew up. Jesus read in the synagogue a passage from the prophet Isaiah that clearly defined his mission on earth:

"THE SPIRIT OF THE LORD IS UPON ME,
BECAUSE HE ANOINTED ME TO PREACH THE GOSPEL TO THE POOR.
HE HAS SENT ME TO PROCLAIM RELEASE TO THE CAPTIVES,
AND RECOVERY OF SIGHT TO THE BLIND,
TO SET FREE THOSE WHO ARE OPPRESSED,
TO PROCLAIM THE FAVORABLE YEAR OF THE LORD" (Luke 4:18-19).

Teaching centered in Christ and directed by the Holy Spirit brings a message of deliverance. This message recovers voice and agency for teachers and students to defend those in need and brings freedom of thought and expression.

## Freedom of Thought and Expression

The Holy Spirit bestows on us freedom of thought and spiritual expression. In Christ, all believers receive the gift of the Holy Spirit by God's grace and not by the works of the law (Gal. 3:2, 5). God gives us complete freedom to serve him that allows us to leave behind the loyalty to legalism regardless of how religiously attractive it might be. The book of Galatians is an excellent testimony about the freedom we have in Christ and the new calling we receive to live in a way that reflects the Holy Spirit's presence in our lives because of Christ sacrifice on our behalf: "It was for freedom that Christ set us free; therefore keep standing firm and do not be subject again to a yoke of slavery" (Gal.

5:1). In this way, Christian teaching brings a message of freedom to all people, beginning with ourselves.

The basis of Christianity is found in the triune God and the redemption work for all humanity. The father loves us unconditionally and receive us as his children (1 John 3:1). The Holy Spirit gives us the liberty to freely live (2 Cor. 3:17). Jesus Christ as the Lord of creation and the Lord of salvation gives us new life together with him (Col. 2:13). Therefore, by God's grace all believers enjoy a relationship with the triune God. Christianity is not established on theological presuppositions or religious laws, but in the triune God that brings us into a relationship with him through the sacrificial work of Christ and the Holy Spirit's guide.

Nevertheless, a general human tendency is the desire to establish religious laws in order to please God. In fact, it can be argued that any religion finds its purpose in human principles with the intention to please a god. For this reason, legalism becomes a logical consequence of any religion. Our Christian faith, however, is not focused on ourselves or our actions, but in God and what he has done for us. Consequently, the Christian life and Christian teaching are established in the freedom of God through the redemptive work of Christ and the ministry of the Holy Spirit.

The temptation to establish rules to regulate believers' behaviors has been present since the beginning of Christianity. God's grace is so supernatural that, unfortunately, it becomes hard to comprehend and accept in our lives. It is easier to limit our understanding of the Christian life to human parameters that we can control and measure, but the new life in Christ is based on the work of God not in ourselves. Just like us, believers in Colossae struggled to integrate their new identity in Christ with their daily lives. In his letter to the Colossians, the apostle Paul concludes in Colossians 2:16-23 his masterful description about the person and work of Christ explaining that in Christ believers now have a new model to imitate that goes beyond any religious practices. We now have the freedom not to follow human stipulations to please God:

> Therefore no one is to act as your judge in regard to food or drink or in respect to a festival or a new moon or a Sabbath day— things which are a *mere* shadow of what is to come; but the substance belongs to Christ. Let no one keep defrauding you of your prize by delighting in self-abasement and the worship of the angels, taking his stand on *visions* he has seen, inflated without cause by his fleshly mind, and not holding fast to the head, from whom the entire body, being supplied and held together by the joints and ligaments, grows with a growth which is from God.

> If you have died with Christ to the elementary principles of the world, why, as if you were living in the world, do you submit yourself to decrees, such as, "Do not handle, do not taste, do not touch!" (which all *refer to* things destined to perish with use)—in accordance with the commandments and teachings of men? These are matters which have, to be sure, the appearance of wisdom in self-made religion and self-abasement and severe treatment of the body, *but are* of no value against fleshly indulgence.

God granted us the liberty from legalistic behavior and we now should live according to the freedom we have in Christ. Legalism focuses on external behavior, but in Christ we are free from wordily regulations. Legalism centers on actions, but the Holy Spirit changes hearts. Human laws appear to be godly and pious, but cannot transform our fleshly desires to please God. The Holy Spirit is the only one who can really change our lives. For this reason, only the Holy Spirit's anointing brings true freedom.

The liberty we have in Christ has implications beyond our conduct. As followers of Christ we now have the freedom of conscience to think and express ourselves. Christian teaching liberates the students to think and pursue truth with complete freedom. United in the essential tenants of the faith, every believer is free to explore ideas and learn from others. Sadly, many Christians tend to stress the secondary differences and personal preferences more than the essentials beliefs of Christianity. Authentic Christian teaching appreciates the diversity in the body of Christ and the different ways in which the Holy Spirit works among believers.

Antonio del Corro (1527-1591) was one of the most important figures in the Spanish Reformation. Del Corro, a Jerome monk like Casiodoro de Reina and Cipriano de Valera, placed his faith in the redemptive work of Christ and he suffered persecution from the Spanish Inquisition. Antonio del Corro was able to flee Spain to escape from the Inquisition, but later on he also faced persecution from different Protestant groups that wanted him to follow their doctrinal positions. In his letter to the Lutheran Pastors in Antwerp, del Corro attempted to reconcile the Lutheran and Calvinist disagreements regarding the Lord's Supper. He called to reject the secondary differences that different groups were trying to elevate as foundational beliefs as if they were a fifth gospel. This rejection was not because these beliefs were not important or irrelevant, but because they did not have the same level of authority as the Scriptures:

There are others who make their confessions, catechisms, commentaries and traditions as if they were a fifth Gospel, and want to authorize their particular interpretations so that they put them at the level of the articles of faith, and they dare to call heretics all those who do not exactly follow their imaginations: which, although they might be good and full of edification, are made by men, and therefore, unworthy to be compared with the word of the Lord.[27]

Nowadays, we can imitate the example of Antonio del Corro to differentiate the message from the Scriptures from our personal opinions and perspectives. The Holy Spirit the divine author of the Bible, the Word of God, and the one who instructs, reproves, corrects, and trains us to walk in divine paths (2 Tim. 3:16). The teaching ministry of the Holy Spirit leads us to the truth of God and gives us freedom to explore and search the Spirit's guidance. Only in the Holy Spirit we can enjoy true liberty!

## Conclusion

We live in difficult times. On the one hand, difficulties and despair seem to be prevalent in our midst. On the other hand, legalism and oppression also continue growing in around us. In the middle of this situation, the Holy Spirit liberates us from any bondage, personal, social or spiritual. The Holy Spirit's anointing allows Christian educators to proclaim the divine message of freedom and flourishing. Christian teaching recovers the voices of students and teachers and invites us to live in complete freedom from human legalism. We can rest and find peace in the Spirit of the living God. The Holy Spirit's message brings refreshment and live to those who listen. Regardless of our circumstances, even in the most difficult ones, we can always rely on the sweet words of the Spirit who reminds us, "The Spirit and the bride say, "Come." And let the one who hears say, "Come." And let the one who is thirsty come; let the one who wishes take the water of life without cost" (Rev. 22:17).

---

[27] Octavio J. Esqueda "La Reforma Española: La Influencia Protestante en México y Latinoamérica" en *Die, spanische Reformation' Sonderwege reformatorischen Gedankengutes in Spanien und Hispanoamerika* Marina Ortrud M. Hertrampf (ed.) (Frankfurt, Peter Lang, 2017), 285.

CHAPTER 3

# Teaching and Freedom of Worship

Robert W. Pazmiño

In considering worship, the first task is to define the nature of worship itself before considering how teaching might hopefully contribute to the freedom of worship in all of life. The definition of worship that has most intrigued me over the years is one proposed by Archbishop William Temple. He said "to worship is to quicken the conscience by the holiness of God, to feed the mind with the truth of God, to purge the imagination by the beauty of God, to devote the will to the purpose of God."[28] Temple's definition suggests a holistic understanding of persons with their conscience, mind, imagination and will fully engaged in a relationship with God their Creator, Redeemer and Sustainer in this life and the next. All of life can be lived in conscious dependence upon God for the very breath of life, joyfully sustained by God's resources for an abundant life offered in Jesus Christ and empowered by the Holy Spirit.

I personally see worship as enabling participants to glorify and fully enjoy God now and forever as the Westminster Confession suggests is the chief end or purpose of persons. Teaching within the Christian tradition fosters the explicit and implicit connections between *lex credenti* (learning aspect of faith) and *lex orandi* (worshipping aspect of faith) in both implicit and explicit ways as Fernando Arzola suggests.[29] Teaching contributes to that glorification of God and joy as experienced by those who can become aware of the divine side of worship with God

---

[28] William Temple, *The Hope of a New World* (London: Student Christian Movement Press, 1941), 30.
[29] Fernando Arzola Jr., Fernando Arzola Jr., *Exploring Worship: Catholic, Evangelical and Orthodox Perspectives* (Eugene, OR: Wipf and Stock, 2011), 93 and also see the discussion in Robert W. Pazmiño, *Foundational Issues in Christian Education*, third ed. (Grand Rapids: Baker Academic, 2008), 51-53 regarding education *for* worship and education *of* worship in relation to the explicit and implicit ways that worship and teaching connect.

as both the object and subject through instruction in the faith.[30] At its best, teaching nurtures our reflection upon the glory of God evident in all of creation, and the gifts of God in Jesus Christ and the Holy Spirit to renew that creation each day.

In a five-task model that I have developed for understanding the purposes of Christian education as inspired by Dr. E. V. Hill during my seminary years, worship stands at the central position (one that I added), pictured at the pitching mound of a softball diamond or at the center of a mandala.[31] The other four purposes are proclamation (first base), community formation (second base), service (third base) and advocacy (home base). To score a run, all four bases must be firmly touched, but the game cannot progress without the ball first being tossed from the pitcher's mound at the center of the diamond. All of the results and fruits of Christian teaching rely upon the connections being made explicit to worship as participants revere the presence of God in all of life, conscious of God's accompaniment. Such an awareness of God leads to adoration and praise. This is the perspective developed in detail in the work of Debra Dean Murphy who proposes that worship itself, as praise and adoration of God, is at the very heart of Christian education. Murphy maintains that Christian education begins and ends with the worship of the triune God most fully revealed in the person and work of Jesus Christ.[32] Therefore, a doxological priority in Christian teaching that seeks to glorify God in all that is done enables education to fulfill its God-intended ultimate end. The challenge for Christian teachers is how this can be possible recognizing all the human constraints and environmental factors present in any educational context. So as not to lose hope, God has provided the person and ministry of the Holy Spirit to partner with human teachers in teaching. The teaching examples of both Jesus and the Apostle Paul can instruct us as Christian teachers.

### Jesus and Photini: Worshipping in Spirit and Truth

Orthodox tradition names the Samaritan woman mentioned in the Gospel of John chapter four as Photini, translated as the "enlightened one" who after encountering Jesus as the anointed one becomes the first evangelist to her village and the first evangelist of this Gospel tradition.

[30] Arzola, 83, as drawn from Robert Webber, *Worship Old and New*, Rev ed. (Grand Rapids: Zondervan, 1994) 262.
[31] Robert W. Pazmiño, *Foundational Issues in Christian Education,* Third ed. (Grand Rapids: Baker Academic, 2008), 46.
[32] Debra Dean Murphy, *Teaching that Transforms: Worship as the Heart of Christian Education* (Grand Rapids: Brazos, 2004), 113.

In his encounter with the Samaritan woman, with Photini, Jesus teaches her about worship:

> But the hour is coming, and is now here, when the true worshippers will worship the Father in spirit and truth, for the Father seeks such as these to worship him. God is spirit, and those who worship him must worship him in spirit and truth. (John 4: 23-24)

The New Testament scholar Raymond Brown insightfully comments on these verses that true worship involves the Spirit of Truth; "the Spirit is the Spirit of Jesus and is the Spirit of Truth (John 14:17; 15:26). God can be worshipped as Father only by those who possess the Spirit that makes them God's children (see Rom 8:15-16), the Spirit by which God begets from above (John 3:5)."[33] In the company of Jesus, Photini embraces a freedom to be herself, and a freedom to be recognized by him and by God for who she was. This enabled her to see Jesus for whom he was, namely the anointed one, the Messiah. This response embraced truth about her person, about God and about the nature of her relationships. Photini is free for genuine worship of Jesus whom she personally encountered.

The Holy Spirit likewise enables us to disclose our identity and to admit our failings and strengths just as was the case for Photini. The Holy Spirit calls for vulnerability and integrity. By being open to a genuine encounter with Jesus, she was empowered to share the significance of her new-found faith with those who may well have despised her or at least, knew her. She was a powerful witness, an evangelist to the Samaritans about Jesus and what he offered to those who lived beyond the Jewish community.

Jesus crossed the borders into Samaria; he crossed the boundaries of usual communication between Jews and Samaritans and between women and men. This border crossing enabled a transformative encounter. In this crossing, he was guided by the Spirit. Photini worshipped by sharing her discovery with her neighbors. The response of those who heard her testimony was remarkable. The freedom to worship God in the person of Jesus, to worship in God in Spirit and truth enabled the liberation of Photini, the celebration of her discovery shared with other Samaritans, and the sustenance of their faith supported by Jesus' staying with them for two days which is a significant commitment:

---

[33] Raymond E. Brown, *The Gospel According to John I-XII* (Garden City, NY: Doubleday, 1966), 180.

Many Samaritans from that city believed in him because of the woman's testimony, "He told me everything I have ever done." So when the Samaritans came to him, they asked him to stay with them; and he stayed there two days. And many more believed because of his word. They said to the woman, "It is no longer because of what you said that we believe, for we have heard for ourselves, and we know that this is truly the savior of the world." (John 4:39-42)

Worship enabled by the Spirit of Truth, by the Spirit of Jesus brings freedom to Photini and to all those Samaritans who encounter Jesus and know for themselves his anointed status and his offer of salvation. Freedom of worship enables us to hear, to see and know the truth in the person of Jesus and to see all of life in the light of that truth. The Samaritans, evangelized by Photini and taught by Jesus for two whole days, worshipped God empowered by the Spirit of truth to experience new life. Christian teaching can support a freedom of worship that enables students to connect personal and communal spiritual life just as was the case for Photini. Photini shared her personal spiritual encounter with others that enabled them to communally respond to the teaching of Jesus. A similar pattern is discerned in the ministry of Paul who mentored both Timothy and Titus following the explicit guidelines of 2 Timothy 2:2: "And what you have heard from me through many witnesses entrust to faithful people who will be able to teach others as well."

## Paul: The Spirit Undergirding Teaching

The Apostle Paul in Romans 8:32 posed a question that can reassure us: "He who did not withhold his own Son, but gave him up for all of us, will he not with him also give us everything else?" That "everything else" includes the coming of the Holy Spirit at Pentecost to empower, equip and sustain Christian teachers in their calling. Paul reassured his teaching mentee Timothy in 2 Tim 1:7: "For God did not give us a spirit of cowardice, but rather a spirit of power and of love and of self-discipline." Another translation refers to "self-discipline" as a "sound mind." Another of Paul's mentees, Titus also needed not be timid is his ministry that included teaching persons of all ages as described in Titus 2:1-15 with its noteworthy heading. The passage describes good household management guided by theological wisdom gifted by God's Spirit[34]:

---

[34]The use of the New Testament Book of Titus as a pastoral epistle may be problematic for Christian feminists who appropriately object to the perceived limited role of women advocated in this section of Scripture as compared with Jesus' explicit affirmation of their ministry as described in the Gospel

But as for you, teach what is consistent with sound doctrine. Tell the older men to be temperate, serious, prudent, and sound in faith, in love, and in endurance.

Likewise, tell the older women to be reverent in behavior, not to be slanderers or slaves to drink; they are to teach what is good, so that they may encourage the young women to love their husbands, to love their children, to be self-controlled, chaste, good managers of the household, kind, being submissive to their husbands, so that the word of God may not be discredited.

Likewise, urge the younger men to be self-controlled. Show yourself in all respects a model of good works, and in your teaching show integrity, gravity, and sound speech that cannot be censured; then any opponent will be put to shame, having nothing evil to say of us.

Tell slaves to be submissive to their masters and to give satisfaction in every respect; they are not to talk back, not to pilfer, but to show complete and perfect fidelity, so that in everything they may be an ornament to the doctrine of God our Savior.

For the grace of God has appeared, bringing salvation to all, training us to renounce impiety and worldly passions, and in the present age to live lives that are self-controlled, upright, and godly, while we wait for the blessed hope and the manifestation of the glory of our great God and Savior, Jesus Christ. He it is who gave himself for us that he might redeem us from all iniquity and purify for himself a people of his own who are zealous for good deeds. Declare these things; exhort and reprove with all authority. Let no one look down on you.

Titus' students shockingly includes slaves and this mention requires our historical perspective that advocates for the full liberation of all persons from all forms of slavery even in the midst of global human trafficking that continues to plague humanity. Children are also not named except as the object of the love of young women. I would add the need for children to receive the love of young men along with old men and old women in their role as members of congregations and families. As a grandparent, I celebrate the mutual love shared with grandchildren that adds a dimension of joy to life as suggested by Psalm 128:6 "May you see your children's children. Peace be upon Israel!" The teaching and love of children is crucial despite the regular reports of misplaced love in the case of epidemic child abuse and neglect with the discouraging complicity of church leadership in that abuse. The cases of

---

accounts. My use of the letter to Titus recognizes the cultural context where women did not have extensive access to education and patriarchal patterns persisted. The contemporary cultural context is distinct and I affirm the full participation of women in teaching ministries at all levels of the Christian church and wider society. See James D. G. Dunn "The First and Second Letters to Timothy and Titus," in *The New Interpreter's Bible* Volume XI (Nashville: Abingdon, 2000), 868-874.

continued slavery and domestic and child abuse in the third millennium require the responses of lament to complement the experiences of joy as appropriate themes for corporate worship. Slavery and abuse are examples of quenching the Spirit about which Christian teachers are clearly warned: "Do not quench the Spirit." (1 Thes 5:19) The willingness to raise awareness and to advocate for victims and perpetrators alike in worship honors the purposes of God in the human family with a call to the end the cycles of oppression and to destroy the destroyers of life. The faithful engagement of Christians with these persistent issues requires spiritual warfare and a partnership with the liberating Spirit who launches efforts in communal worship that are sustained throughout each week by Christian disciples in their personal, communal and corporate lives.

With these particular provisos regarding the Titus passage and contemporary applications, teaching is affirmed as a passing on of wisdom for living and the formation of character regarding how folk should be and become. Living in faithful households of families and congregations required reliance upon God's Spirit to reflect the virtues of the Christian faith in daily living. All of life is to be lived for the glory of God and all of life can be seen as an act of worship.

Making the connections between faith and life requires instruction that Titus is encouraged to give recognizing the needs of distinct age groups, but more importantly to live out himself. The living out of the faith as an act of worship honors the key role of social learning, modeling and mentoring for the sustenance of the Christian household or community. Freedom is realized in fulfilling God's design for faithful human relationships that require definition in each cultural context. Freedom suggests the place of ardor, passion and joy, but is always complemented in human life with the place of form and order given the created nature of life. Worship itself enables the gaining of perspective with God as the subject who enlightens our conscience, mind, imagination and will with the exemplar of Jesus our Lord whom we follow and with the tutor of the Holy Spirit who empowers and guides our steps.

The perichoretic dance of the triune God invites our full participation in worship as the object of our reverence, wonder and awe. That dance extends into our daily living for as Paul suggests: "If we live by the Spirit, let us also be guided by or walk by the Spirit." (Gal 5:25) Living by the Spirit in worship, in theological understanding and in sound doctrine, calls us to walking by the Spirit in our household and public interactions and relationships guided by the Spirit's promptings. In Hispanic life, the matter of *lo cotidiano* (or everyday life) emerges as central to how a Spirit-filled life issues in everyday living and seeing just as Titus was instructed by Paul to live and teach. Titus suggests guidelines for daily living in the household of faith.

## Implications for Teaching

The work of Maria Harris is instructive for exploring freedom of worship in the very forms of teaching while discerning an underlying dance of the Spirit. Harris draws upon the work of Michele Russell who identifies seven methodological principles as critical in teaching:

1. Take one subject at a time
2. Encourage story-telling
3. Give political value to daily life
4. Be able to speak in tongues
5. Use everything
6. Be concrete
7. Have a dream.[35]

These principles allow space for the Spirit to work and speak through the lives of participants and teachers alike, and to explore the implications for the context of our living that balances ideals and realities in a creative rhythm. This teaching rhythm echoes the rhythm of our breathing in and out to sustain life and to live it abundantly as the Spirit infused our bodies from the creation to become living spirits. Continued life in the Spirit requires an awareness of the logic of the Spirit of which James Loder researched and wrote.

## Loder on the Spirit

James Loder researched the process of spiritual transformation and suggested five steps that characterize its experience by persons. Freedom of worship in teaching enables the possibility of spiritual transformation. The five steps provide guideposts for teaching practice that seeks to invite persons to be open to transformation made possible by God's Spirit.[36] Transformation in Christian perspective can be seen as a work of the Holy Spirit upon the spirits, hearts, and lives of persons in the third millennium. From the perspective of Christian theology this can apply

---

[35] Maria Harris, *Women and Teaching* (New York: Paulist Press, 1988), 65

[36] See James E. Loder, *The Logic of the Spirit: Human Development in Theological Perspective* (San Francisco: Jossey-Bass, 1998), and his earlier work James E. Loder, *The Transforming Moment: Understanding Convictional Experiences,* 2nd ed. (Colorado Springs: Helmers & Howard, 1989), 3-4.

both to Christian education and general education of the public. It can also apply to education in other religious traditions through the operation of common grace and general revelation as an aspect of God's plenitude, which is the abundant fullness of God's grace.[37] Such a claim affirms the place of special grace and revelation that Christians celebrate in Jesus Christ and the continuing ministry of the Spirit. It also affirms the universality of the cosmic Christ, the Spirit's work in all of creation and God's goodness manifest in a variety of forms.[38] Christian teaching can embrace the particularity of the Christian Gospel and its universalistic implications for teaching of the common good for all of creation. In theological terms, both the creative and redemptive covenants of God are affirmed for Christian teachers in the third millennium postmodern context made possible through the coming of the Holy Spirit at Pentecost. Postmodern developments invite a wider engagement of Christian theology with the public realities of God's creation and the interplay between Christians and non-Christians in the search for truth that preoccupies education in general, and religious education in particular.[39] Loder's work on the process of spiritual transformation provides insights for Christian teachers and possible connections with the work of other religious educators who are also committed to the processes of transformation in education.

## Loder's Five Steps of Transformation

The five steps Loder identifies for transformations are the following: conflict in context; interlude for scanning; insight felt with intuitive force; release and repatterning; and interpretation and verification. Each of these steps can be directly related to teaching as I have discussed in *Basics of Teaching for Christians*.[40] In summarizing that earlier discussion, I suggest that for the first step of conflict in context a teacher can invite transformation by posing questions and problems for persons. As Abraham Heschel observed "religion begins with a question and that theology begins with a problem."[41] Engaging persons requires their participation in the process of critical inquiry and searching for truth

---

[37] See S. Mark Heim, The *Depth of the Riches: A Trinitarian Theology of Religious Ends* (Grand Rapids: Eerdmans, 2000), 123-296 for a discussion of the plenitude of God's grace.
[38] See my discussion of religious pluralism in *By What Authority Do We Teach?: Sources for Empowering Christian Educators* (Eugene, Ore.: Wipf and Stock, 2002), 119-46.
[39] Pazmiño, *God Our Teacher*, 161-72.
[40] Loder, *Transforming Moment*, 3-4. I discuss the relationship between each of these steps and teaching in Robert W. Pazmiño, *Basics of Teaching for Christians: Preparation, Instruction, and Evaluation* (Eugene, Ore.: Wipf and Stock, 2002), 61-62.
[41] Reuven Kimelman, "Abraham Joshua Heschel: Our Generation's Teacher in Honor of the Tenth Yahrzeit," *Religion and Intellectual Life* 2 (Winter 1985): 17.

which a question and/or problem can invite. The Spirit invites us to consider what comes next? This first step also requires of the teacher sensitivity to the present and wider context of persons for their perception of a connection to their settings and lives. Conflicts are not avoided in the first step, but are carefully confronted for what they can offer. Conflict can provide space for the Spirit to work.

The second step of an interlude for scanning fosters a safe and hospitable space for exploration that provides viable options for consideration. Scanning presupposes openness to new perspectives and possibilities not previously considered and occasioned by the question or problem posed. New voices can be heard and responded to in the process of scanning. Scanning assumes receptivity and openness to transformation that engages the spiritual imagination. We can explore what new ventures is the Spirit inviting us to consider?

The third step of insight felt with intuitive force is the breakthrough or enlightening that for the person of faith involves the work of God's grace in persons' lives. For Christians this step honors the person and ministry of the Holy Spirit who works in partnership with the spirits of the teacher and students in an educational setting. Wisdom is discerned or discovered and moves the heart, soul, and body in addition to the mind in receiving the gracious gift of insight. Insight is a gift of the Holy Spirit. "Outsight," to coin a term, can complement insight that calls for seeing the wider world through Spirit's eyes or from God's perspective seen in the light of creation, redemption and consummation.

The fourth step of release and repatterning supports the integration of the new insight into the framework of persons' world and life views with a holistic appropriation of the truth. As the new treasure is brought forth from the storehouse of God's plentitude, the old treasure as well is seen in a new light and with deeper appreciation (Matt 13:52). Spiritual discernment is required to balance the old and new in such a way that growth and not distortion is achieved.

The fifth step of interpretation and verification allows for the wider sharing and dissemination of the wisdom personally gained with one's various relationships and associations. Here is the bearing of witness to what God's Spirit has accomplished in the lives of individuals, communities and the wider society. The end of this process is new life in spiritual terms that brings integration, wholeness and holiness that the scriptures discuss in terms of *shalom* that God intends for all of creation and humanity.

Loder's steps provide suggestive insights rather than a rigid programming of the work of the Holy Spirit who delights to bring surprise and wonder into human experience. These steps do provide hints for how the human teacher can be open to the person and work of the Holy Spirit in the ordinary rhythms of teaching and learning. The teacher must also be flexible to allow God's Spirit to draw upon the spirit of each person both within and outside the times set apart for instruction. The teacher also needs to honor the teaching and learning that is nurtured among participants where persons learn much from peers in their interactions and dialogue. By nurturing spiritual transformation in partnership with the Spirit, teachers honor the freedom of worship in their teaching and the learning they seek to foster in the lives of students. Theology informs us regarding the key role that worship plays in all of life that includes our educational life in community.

## A Theological Capstone to Consider

Miroslav Volf suggests that "the key to our true human identity is our communion with God through the Spirit."[42] Worship provides the special activity that nurtures that communion and also infuses all of life's activities, including teaching. Volf elaborates:

> No doubt, Christians should worship God with their whole existence, work included (see Rom. 12:1f.). As they serve God through their work, they worship God. But God did not create human beings simply to be servants but above all to be God's children and friends. As much as they need to do God's will, so also they need to enjoy God's presence. In order to be truly who they are, they need periodic moments of time in which God's commands and their tasks will disappear from the forefront of their consciousness and in which God will be there for them and they will be there for God—to adore the God of loving holiness and to thank and pray to the God of holy love. It is the union of human beings with the Son of God through the Spirit (see 1 Cor. 1:9). Paul describes this union with metaphors that underscore its most intimate nature, such as the metaphor of "being made to drink" of the Spirit (1 Cor. 12:13). When Christians commune with God in worship, they come to drink from that fountain their very life as Christians and hence their identity as human beings depends on. At the same time, in worship they anticipate the enjoyment of God in the new creation where they will communally dwell in the triune God and the triune God will dwell in them (see Rev. 21:22; John 17:21).[43]

Teaching that connects with worship and nurtures the freedom of worship, embraces a Christian identity as a child of God, a follower and

---

[42] Miroslav Volf, *Work in the Spirit* (New York: Oxford University Press, 1991), 136.
[43] Ibid, 137.

disciple of Jesus Christ and a partner with the Holy Spirit both in this life and in the life to come. This chapter emphasizes that teaching at its best can nurture communion with God through the Spirit and embrace the highest freedom afforded to participants. Christian teaching, as Archbishop Temple suggested, can quicken the conscience, mind, imagination and will with all the wonders of God in partnership with the Holy Spirit. What a delight.

# CHAPTER 4

# Teaching and Freedom From Want

Robert W. Pazmiño

Freedom from want raises the pressing issues poverty and hunger on the global scale and the response of persons of faith. The question of sufficiency of resources to address global, national, regional and local needs looms in relation to real needs of people as distinguished from the wants promoted by a culture of materialism and consumerism. A freedom from want suggests the basic human needs of food, portable water, clothing and shelter and the corresponding access to medical, educational, legal, safety and vocational resources necessary to sustain life. The sustainability of current levels of global consumption of basic resources raises the matter of stewardship of God's creation and the equitable resource distribution for generations to come. The Amerindian value considers the legacy left for seven generations to come in the light of current policies and practices. The emergence of green theologies in Christian communities relates faith questions to how we view the creation and its critical care in the light of a global ecological crisis. Some discount the crisis despite the overwhelming scientific evidence supporting the realities of climate change and sea-level increases that contribute to recent natural disasters like Hurricane Sandy that devastated coastal areas of New York and New Jersey where I and my wife visited in the summer of 2012.

FDR in his "Four Freedoms Speech" in 1941 to the U. S. nation proposed "a freedom from want for everyone everywhere in the world" that was and still is a lofty goal. The work of the United Nations in terms of eight millennium development goals provided greater specificity as nations across the globe have attempted to address and work for change that requires the cooperation and collaboration of a wide variety of nations and groups. The 17 Sustainable Development Goals for 2030 are the following that are a worth continued consideration and commitment on the part of Christians:

Goal 1.     End poverty in all its forms everywhere
Goal 2.     End hunger, achieve food security and improved nutrition and promote sustainable agriculture
Goal 3.     Ensure healthy lives and promote well-being for all at all ages
Goal 4.     Ensure inclusive and equitable quality education and promote lifelong learning opportunities for all
Goal 5.     Achieve gender equality and empower all women and girls
Goal 6.     Ensure availability and sustainable management of water and sanitation for all
Goal 7.     Ensure access to affordable, reliable, sustainable and modern energy for all
Goal 8.     Promote sustained, inclusive and sustainable economic growth, full and productive employment and decent work for all
Goal 9.     Build resilient infrastructure, promote inclusive and sustainable industrialization and foster innovation
Goal 10.    Reduce inequality within and among countries
Goal 11.    Make cities and human settlements inclusive, safe, resilient and sustainable
Goal 12.    Ensure sustainable consumption and production patterns
Goal 13.    Take urgent action to combat climate change and its impacts
Goal 14.    Conserve and sustainably use the oceans, seas and marine resources for sustainable development
Goal 15.    Protect, restore and promote sustainable use of terrestrial ecosystems, sustainably manage forests, combat desertification, and halt and reverse land degradation and halt biodiversity loss
Goal 16.    Promote peaceful and inclusive societies for sustainable development, provide access to justice for all and build effective, accountable and inclusive institutions at all levels
Goal 17.    Strengthen the means of implementation and revitalize the global partnership for sustainable development

Such an effort suggests the need for ecumenical, interfaith and even common human cooperation and collaboration given the depth of human suffering and need globally.

My journey to Latin America during a nine-month sabbatical with my family enabled me to see national and global challenges in a totally new light in assessing the impacts of international policies on the lives of persons and families in Central America.[44] The Bible's discussion of

---

[44] Robert W. Pazmiño, *Latin American Journey: Insights for Christian Education in North America* (Cleveland: United Church Press, 1994).

poverty provides perspective on Christian responses. Throughout the Old and New Testaments of the Christian Bible we discover mention of the poor and the realities of poverty often in connection with God's concern for justice and righteousness in human affairs that too often is not the experience for those on the margins of communities. Consider the vision of the psalmist who longed for a time when "Steadfast love and faithfulness will meet; righteousness and peace will kiss each other." (Psalm 85:10) When justice or righteousness and peace embrace or kiss, blessings are shared with all of humanity and all of creation that longs for such a time as Paul made explicit in Romans 8: 18-30:

> I consider that the sufferings of this present time are not worth comparing with the glory about to be revealed to us. For the creation waits with eager longing for the revealing of the children of God; for the creation was subjected to futility, not of its own will but by the will of the one who subjected it, in hope that the creation itself will be set free from its bondage to decay and will obtain the freedom of the glory of the children of God. We know that the whole creation has been groaning in labor pains until now; and not only the creation, but we ourselves, who have the first fruits of the Spirit, groan inwardly while we wait for adoption, the redemption of our bodies. For in hope we were saved. Now hope that is seen is not hope. For who hopes for what is seen? But if we hope for what we do not see, we wait for it with patience.
>
> Likewise the Spirit helps us in our weakness; for we do not know how to pray as we ought, but that very Spirit intercedes with sighs too deep for words. And God, who searches the heart, knows what is the mind of the Spirit, because the Spirit intercedes for the saints according to the will of God.
>
> We know that all things work together for good for those who love God, who are called according to his purpose. For those whom he foreknew he also predestined to be conformed to the image of his Son, in order that he might be the firstborn within a large family. And those whom he predestined he also called; and those whom he called he also justified; and those whom he justified he also glorified.

The Spirit's intercessory ministry sustains Christians in their callings who hopefully await "the redemption of our bodies." What about the current condition of the bodies, not only of Christians, but of everyone in the world in the light of this future glory and the presence of the poor who are always with us (John 12:8)?

Why should the concern for "freedom from want" concern Christians as they await a future glory secured by God's Spirit? The social responsibility of Jesus' followers warrants further explanation if

Christian teachers are to teach their students in this area of social ministry. Paul instructed Timothy about caring for others: "And whoever does not provide for relatives, and especially for family members, has denied the faith and is worse than an unbeliever." (1 Tim 5:8) But what about unbelievers can be asked? Do they warrant the care and concern of believers for their bodies as well as their souls? Galatians 6:10 suggests a broader social commitment: "So then, whenever we have an opportunity, let us work for the good of all, and especially for those of the family of faith." The "all" here encompasses all of humanity and is supported by our theological anthropological understanding, our understanding of human persons created in God's image. The *Lausanne Covenant* described the doctrine of man or persons this way: "Because of every person's inherent dignity as a godlike being, (s)he should be respected and served, indeed loved (Lev. 19:18; Luke 6:27, 35), not exploited."[45] This foundational biblical understanding enables a response to all forms of oppression like racism, sexism and social prejudice that deny the worth and dignity of persons as made in God's image. Oppression systematically limits the access of resources to certain persons and groups based upon their differences. To insult persons in these ways and to deny their basic needs is "to blaspheme God." (James 3:9, 10)[46] The problem with differences is that they are viewed as deficiencies in the wider culture of the United States with historical patterns perpetuating prejudice, power and privilege for those viewed as insiders to the exclusion of outsiders.[47]

Honoring the voices of the poor, those marginalized and oppressed known as the *anawim* is essential to welcome all to the metaphorical table of teaching that follows Jesus' example. The *anawim* are those who are poor, humble, or weak before God and others and often represent outsiders in our communities. By virtue of our created nature with sin and suffering, all persons may see themselves at some point in their lives as one of the *anawim*. But some folk because of the systemic forces of racism, sexism, classism, ageism and a host of oppressions, experience this outsider status on a persistent daily basis. In relation to the wider societal and structural forces of oppression, Christian teachers are called to engage a spiritual warfare that rebukes in the name of Jesus principalities and powers that oppress. (Eph 6:10-20) No persons are to

---

[45] John Stott, *The Lausanne Covenant: An Exposition and Commentary* (Minneapolis: World Wide Publications, 1975), 27

[46] Ibid.

[47] See the discussion of insiders and outsiders in Jesus' teaching ministry in Robert W. Pazmiño, *So What Makes Our Teaching Christian?: Teaching in the Name, Spirit, and Power of Jesus* (Eugene, Ore.: Wipf and Stock, 2008), 95-106.

remain under the physical and metaphorical table and excluded from the feast shared at the invitation of Jesus. As the gift of loaves and fishes are prayed over with thanksgiving and multiplied with twelve baskets leftover in feeding hungry persons (Matt 12:13-21; Mark 6:30-44; Luke 9:10-17; John 6:1-14), so Christian teachers need to advocate for full access to the teaching and other resources available to them and distributed inequitably in many communities. The Christian teacher is called to be attentive to those on the margins and to ministry in all areas of life extending God's love in Christ in concrete ways. The discoveries of Gustavo Gutierrez in working with the poor are helpful in understanding how this might be done. José Miguez Bonino summarized Gutierrez's account of his discoveries:

> I discovered three things. I discovered that poverty was a destructive thing, something to be fought against and destroyed, not merely something which was the object of our charity. Secondly, I discovered that poverty was not accidental. The fact that these people are poor and not rich is not just a matter of chance, but the result of a structure. It was a structural question. Thirdly, I discovered that poor people were a social class. When I discovered that poverty was something to be fought against, that poverty was structural, that poor people were a class, it became crystal clear that in order to serve the poor, one had to move into political action.[48]

Political action can be a means to address Jesus' love and concern for the poor in concrete ways as exemplified in his earthly ministries of feeding and healing.

Two key historical works of the last century that posed the issues of want for Protestant and evangelical Christians in particular, were *Rich Christians in an Age of Hunger* (1977) by Ronald J. Sider and *The Mustard Seed Conspiracy* (1981) by Tom Sine.[49] These works fully documented God's persistent concern for the poor in the scriptures and the gap existing in the practices of Christians. In the United States, a persistent prophetic voice in relation to the Protestant community has been that of Jim Wallis and the Sojourners ministry. The legacy of Dorothy Day and the Catholic Worker movement has been a longer standing voice in the Catholic community. All of these voices have nurtured a recovery of Jesus' legacy and teaching in relation to the poor

---

[48] José Miguez Bonino, "Statement by José Miguez Bonino," in *Theology in the Americas*, eds. Sergio Torres and John Eagleson (Maryknoll, N. Y.: Orbis, 1976), 278.

[49] See Ronald J. Sider, *Rich Christians in an Age of Hunger: A Biblical Study* (Downers Grove, Ill.: InterVarsity Press, 1977); and Tom Sine, *The Mustard Seed Conspiracy* (Waco, Tex.: Word Books, 1981).

and how to honor a freedom from want among the least of these as Jesus' brothers and sisters across the globe who daily struggle for sustenance. Jesus' concern for the poor and marginated is evident in his teaching.

The fifth and final teaching block or unit from the Gospel according to Matthew outlines Jesus' sobering teaching on the judgment of the nations in relation to their response to human want:

> "When the Son of Man comes in his glory, and all the angels with him, then he will sit on the throne of his glory. All the nations will be gathered before him, and he will separate people one from another as a shepherd separates the sheep from the goats, and he will put the sheep at his right hand and the goats at the left. Then the king will say to those at his right hand, 'Come, you that are blessed by my Father, inherit the kingdom prepared for you from the foundation of the world; for I was hungry and you gave me food, I was thirsty and you gave me something to drink, I was a stranger and you welcomed me, I was naked and you gave me clothing, I was sick and you took care of me, I was in prison and you visited me.' Then the righteous will answer him, 'Lord, when was it that we saw you hungry and gave you food, or thirsty and gave you something to drink? And when was it that we saw you a stranger and welcomed you, or naked and gave you clothing? And when was it that we saw you sick or in prison and visited you?' And the king will answer them, 'Truly I tell you, just as you did it to one of the least of these who are members of my family, you did it to me.' Then he will say to those at his left hand, 'You that are accursed, depart from me into the eternal fire prepared for the devil and his angels; for I was hungry and you gave me no food, I was thirsty and you gave me nothing to drink, I was a stranger and you did not welcome me, naked and you did not give me clothing, sick and in prison and you did not visit me.' Then they also will answer, 'Lord, when was it that we saw you hungry or thirsty or a stranger or naked or sick or in prison, and did not take care of you?' Then he will answer them, 'Truly I tell you, just as you did not do it to one of the least of these, you did not do it to me.' And these will go away into eternal punishment, but the righteous into eternal life" (Matt. 25:31-46).

The scenario poses challenges for those who dismiss social concerns from the Christian agenda and disregard the extent of poverty and want that grip persons across the globe. Teachers, at the very least, need to raise the consciousness, the awareness of their students about the extent and causes of human alienation and need. One Christian education approach identified as "Doing the Word" proposes a fourfold sequence of learning to address social needs that includes: awareness, analysis, action and reflection.[50] In a similar sequence, Catholic social tradition proposed a sequence of seeing, judging and acting to move a Christian audience in response to desperate social conditions plaguing humanity. The love of God (the first great commandment) constrains Christians to love their neighbors in concrete and visible ways (the second great commandment) in obeying all the Jesus himself commanded, taught, and lived out in his earthly ministry (Matt 28: 20). His example of caring for and healing the *anawim* poses a challenge for solely individualistic approaches that fail to consider the wider social fabric of life.

## Political Matters and Educational Equity

Addressing freedom from want on a global, national and/or local level engages political life. An exploration of political theology is important, though some suggest it is suspect in relation to spiritual life. If Christians take seriously the implications of the creation as gifted by the Spirit as Lord and Giver of Life, then the sustenance of life requires engagement with political realities in this world. Following Aristotle, politics can be viewed as the art of keeping persons truly human and from a spiritual perspective, truly human as God intended from the creation until the consummation. Jim Wallis is his writing is audacious enough to consider the arena of God's politics as others have considered Jesus' politics in their writings.[51] For the purpose of this text, the questions can be posed: Is there a politics of the Holy Spirit? If so, what characterizes the Spirit's politics?

The most explicit statement of the Spirit's politics might be found in Jesus' own teaching as he launched his ministry in the synagogue at Nazareth:

> "The Spirit of the Lord is upon me,
> because he has anointed me
> to bring good news to the poor.
> He has sent me to proclaim release to the captives
> and recovery of sight to the blind,
> to let the oppressed go free,
> to proclaim the year of the Lord's favor." (Luke 4:18-19)

---

[50] See Sara Little, *To Set One's Heart: Belief and Teaching in the Church* (Atlanta: John Knox, 1983), 80-81; and Charles R. McCollough, *Morality of Power: A Notebook on Christian Education for Social Change* (New York: United Church Press, 1977), 11-18.

[51] Jim Wallis, *God's Politics: Why the Right Gets It Wrong and the Left Doesn't Get It* (San Francisco: Harper San Francisco, 2005) and John H. Yoder, *The Politics of Jesus: Vicit Agnus Noster* (Grand Rapids: Eerdmans, 1972).

Addressing the wants or genuine needs of the poor, the captives, the blind and the oppressed in Jesus' ministry is connected with the Spirit's anointing and demonstrated in Jesus' caring and healing work among a wide variety of people who encountered him. Here he is quoting from Isaiah 61:1-2; and 58:6 with a vision of God's deliverance of humanity and the true worship of doing justice that God expects. The Davidic connection of Jesus' legacy warrants his embrace of the political implications of his anointed teaching in line with what the psalmist longs for in terms of office of king:

> Give the king your justice, O God,
> and your righteousness to a king's son.
> May he judge your people with righteousness,
> and your poor with justice.
> May the mountains yield prosperity for the people,
> and the hills, in righteousness.
> May he defend the cause of the poor of the people,
> give deliverance to the needy,
> and crush the oppressor.

If Jesus serves as prophet, priest and king for Christians today, then the Spirit's teaching curriculum in the ministry of Jesus has import for those who follow Jesus as his disciples. The challenge is posed in how this actually plays out for Christian teachers and their communities in the affairs of human life. The political policies, structures and practices of Christians requires dialogue, interpretation and civility in confronting differences in political affiliation and practice among believers and among citizens alike in any political body. The body politic greatly influences how education is practiced and who has access to educational resources over their lifetime. The pattern of privilege in relation to access to educational resources clearly indicates inequities.[52] In terms of freedom from want, the issue of educational equity emerges for Christians in the United States and globally.

Educational equity can be defined in terms of access to educational resources, respect of difference, space to be heard, the presence of appropriate role models, and shared power and authority at all levels of educational programs in representative proportion.[53]

---

[52] See as one example, Jonathan Kozol, *Savage Inequalities: Children in America's Schools* (New York: Crown, 1991).

[53] Robert W. Pazmiño, *Latin American Journey: Insights for Christian Education in North America* (Cleveland: United Church Press, 1994), 84, 117.

Such a definition of equity is an ideal that calls for the expression of love in the social sphere of our lives. Love in the social sphere embodies justice along with a concern for righteousness in all human relationships. Loving persons in the public and social sphere requires addressing those conditions that prevent a just and equitable life for all of God's children. Love involves caring enough to confront patterns of exclusion and injustice that historically have plagued educational institutions and structures. The impacts of racism, sexism, classism and other forms of oppression have ravaged the educational opportunities and experiences of far too many persons and groups. The loving response to these realities calls for seeing that one of the tasks of teaching is to confront the destroyers of life. These destroyers are manifest in different forms that call for spiritual engagement to make a concrete difference for the "common good" (1 Cor 12:7). Teachers are called to love and care enough to speak up and act.[54]

Teachers create a space where educational and spiritual imaginations are nurtured to explore alternatives that fulfill God's intentions and Jesus' politics as proclaimed at the Nazarene synagogue. The fruits of anointed teaching discussed in this work identify liberation, celebration sustenance and justice as fruits with political dimensions and worthy of the attention and advocacy of Christian teachers. Such fruits have direct implications for works of justice, righteousness and peace building in human life both this side and the other side of heaven.[55]

Abraham Heschel provides some helpful warnings in any discussion of "want" given the impact of consumerism and materialism evident in global society and political affairs:

The mention of genuine or real needs as compared with felt needs is crucial. The Jewish educator Abraham Heschel made this explicit in his warning about the "tyranny of needs" that can plague contemporary perceptions.[56] By this term, Heschel referred to the cultural development whereby felt needs become holy to the relative exclusion of God's demands and human responsibilities. Wants fueled by the idolatries and excesses of consumerism become equated with needs to the peril of creation and its care. Needs identified in typical educational

---

[54] Robert W. Pazmiño, *So What Makes Our Teaching Christian: Teaching in the Name, Spirit and Power of Jesus* (Eugene, Ore.: Wipf and Stock, 2008), 38-39.

[55] See Ellen Ott Marshall, ed. *Choosing Peace Through Daily Practices* (Cleveland: Pilgrim, 2005). This work includes a chapter by Elizabeth Conde-Frazier entitled, "A Spiritual Journey toward Peaceful Living: From Hospitality to Shalom," 158-185.

[56] Abraham J. Heschel, *Between God and Man: An Interpretation of Judaism from the Writings of Abraham Heschel*, ed. Fritz Rothschild (New York: Free Press, 1959), 129-51. Also see Victor Gross, *Educating to Reverence: The Legacy of Abraham Heschel* (Bristol, Ind.: Wyndham Hall, 1989).

planning require spiritual discernment to maintain faithfulness to Jesus' legacy and spirit.[57]

Heschel's warnings are worth heeding while honoring his life's legacy in confronting injustice and racial oppression and calling political leaders to account for their actions and inactions. The distribution and redistribution of resources was evident in the first followers of Jesus as noted in the following account from the Book of Acts:

Now when they heard this, they were cut to the heart and said to Peter and to the other apostles, "Brothers, what should we do?" Peter said to them, "Repent, and be baptized every one of you in the name of Jesus Christ so that your sins may be forgiven; and you will receive the gift of the Holy Spirit. For the promise is for you, for your children, and for all who are far away, everyone whom the Lord our God calls to him." And he testified with many other arguments and exhorted them, saying, "Save yourselves from this corrupt generation." So those who welcomed his message were baptized, and that day about three thousand persons were added. They devoted themselves to the apostles' teaching and fellowship, to the breaking of bread and the prayers.
    Awe came upon everyone, because many wonders and signs were being done by the apostles. All who believed were together and had all things in common; they would sell their possessions and goods and distribute the proceeds to all, as any had need. Day by day, as they spent much time together in the temple, they broke bread at home and ate their food with glad and generous hearts, praising God and having the goodwill of all the people. And day by day the Lord added to their number those who were being saved. (Acts 2:37-47)

The Book of Acts can be identified as the Gospel of the Spirit with the Holy Spirit as the primary agent bringing new life to the followers of Jesus after his death, resurrection and ascension.[58] The description in chapter two suggests an ideal of communal life, but this was soon tested with division and dissention as described in the case of Ananias and Sapphira in Acts 5 and the conflict between Hellenists and Hebrews in Acts 6. Nevertheless, the commitment to address freedom from want is remarkable in this first century context:

Now the whole group of those who believed were of one heart and soul, and no one claimed private ownership of any possessions, but everything they owned was held in common. With great power the apostles gave their testimony to the resurrection of the Lord Jesus, and

---

[57] Pazmiño, So What, 80.
[58] Justo L. González, Acts; The Gospel of the Spirit (Maryknoll, NY: Orbis, 2001).

great grace was upon them all. There was not a needy person among them, for as many as owned lands or houses sold them and brought the proceeds of what was sold. They laid it at the apostles' feet, and it was distributed to each as any had need. There was a Levite, a native of Cyprus, Joseph, to whom the apostles gave the name Barnabas (which means "son of encouragement"). He sold a field that belonged to him, then brought the money, and laid it at the apostles' feet (Acts 4:32-37).

The communal commitment found expression in an operational theology of relinquishment of possessions to meet genuine social needs. Social ministry was embraced by the followers of Jesus' Way. This ministry was at the communal level and the translation of such commitments to larger political bodies, policies and practices presents an ongoing challenge in human and political affairs. The willingness to share possessions requires the work of the Holy Spirit upon human hearts and systemic supports for redistribution. Given their egocentric world view, preschoolers in some cases may be challenged to share their possessions. But they can also be remarkably generous. When egocentrism becomes the pattern of living within a narcissistic culture, adults and youth are similarly challenged to share with their neighbors whom Jesus defined as anyone in need in the Parable of the Good Samaritan (Luke 10:25-37).

The sharing of possessions becomes a challenge for all persons across the socio-economic spectrum with special reference to those of us as privileged on the global scale and rich by worldly standards. Jesus' words to the rich ruler in Luke 18:18-30 are applicable to us today:

A certain ruler asked him, "Good Teacher, what must I do to inherit eternal life?" Jesus said to him, "Why do you call me good? No one is good but God alone. You know the commandments: 'You shall not commit adultery; You shall not murder; You shall not steal; You shall not bear false witness; Honor your father and mother.'" He replied, "I have kept all these since my youth." When Jesus heard this, he said to him, "There is still one thing lacking. Sell all that you own and distribute the money to the poor, and you will have treasure in heaven; then come, follow me." But when he heard this, he became sad; for he was very rich. Jesus looked at him and said, "How hard it is for those who have wealth to enter the kingdom of God! Indeed, it is easier for a camel to go through the eye of a needle than for someone who is rich to enter the kingdom of God." Those who heard it said, "Then who can be saved?" He replied, "What is impossible for mortals is possible for God."

Then Peter said, "Look, we have left our homes and followed you." And he said to them, "Truly I tell you, there is no one who has left house or wife or brothers or parents or children, for the sake of the kingdom of God, who will not get back very much more in this age, and in the age to come eternal life."

The rich ruler was saddened with the implications of Jesus' teaching for his life and the challenge for rich Christians persists today in the light of the plight of the poor globally. The freedom from want that FDR proposed in his "Four Freedoms" speech calls for the stewardship of global resources contrary to the persistent patterns of acquisition supported by a culture of consumerism and materialism prominent in the United States, but embraced globally via a marketing and media oriented network that serves as the primary educator for children, youth and adults. Therefore the Spirit's work towards freedom from want requires a countercultural stance. In this case Jesus can serve as the liberator from our dependencies and affections, all of which tie us down just as the rich ruler, and calling us to embrace a spirit of relinquishment.[59] For Christian teachers to address a freedom from want with our students, the Psalmist's insights are applicable:

Restore to me the joy of your salvation,
and sustain in me a willing spirit.
Then I will teach transgressors your ways,
and sinners will return to you. (Psalm 51: 12-13)

Recognizing the common sin of acquisition and materialism requires the Holy Spirit to speak to our human spirits resulting in our repentance and a restoration of joy in giving and serving even to the point of sacrifice. But a warning needs to be made in relation to sacrifice, issued by Carol Lakey Hess. She notes that "pride is not always a sin and self-sacrifice sometimes is" because "self-development is a higher duty then self-sacrifice."[60] Pride is not always a sin especially for those marginalized and self-sacrifice has too often been an expectation set upon women and girls in diverse cultures given sexism and patriarchal patterns. It is also important to note that poverty and want are actually greater for women and children in the global scheme of resource allotment. Teaching and freedom from want call for a prophetic and subversive stance in Christian teaching begun by Jesus at Nazareth and passed on to his followers.

---

[59] Alan R. Rudnick, "Lessons from a Donkey," in *Lent; Christian Reflection* (Waco, TX: The Center for Christian Ethics at Baylor University, 2013), 76
[60] Carol Lakey Hess, *Caretakers of Our Common House: Women's Development in Communities of Faith* (Nashville: Abingdon, 1997), 38.

CHAPTER 5

# Teaching and Freedom from Fear
Octavio J. Esqueda

Life is tough. As we pay attention to the world around us, we can easily notice the many bad circumstances people face today. This generation now lives in the era of global terrorism with all the tragic consequences and implications it brings to our society like the constant security at airports and strategic public locations. The political landscape in the world is constantly moving to extreme positions with people finding disappointment with traditional perspectives and politicians. Racial tensions continue with rampant growth in our society. Even with the best medical technology in human history, illnesses like cancer continue affecting millions of people around the world. Accordingly, Elie Wiesel, a 1986 Nobel Peace Prize laureate, said: "When I look around the world I see nothing but hopelessness. And yet I must, we all must, try to find a source of hope. We must believe in human beings, in spite of human beings."[61] Life is a constant encounter with unfulfilled expectations that leaves many people in silent desolation and anxiety.

In a climate of fear and despair, hope is essential for all of us. A common expression states the importance of hope in the following way, "human beings can live for forty days without food, four days without water, and four minutes without air. But we cannot live for four seconds without hope."[62] Freedom from fear requires hope, but this confidence is more than wishful thinking or just a positive attitude towards life. It requires a trusted source, a foundation that guarantees our positive expectations. For this reason, Jürgen Moltmann in *Theology of Hope* rightly declares: "Hope is nothing else than the expectation of those things which faith has believed to have been truly promised by God."[63]

---

[61] Robert Franciosi (ed.), *Elie Wiesel: Conversations* (Jackson, MS.: University Press of Mississippi, 2002), 146.
[62] Andy Crouch, "The Gospel of Steve Jobs." *Christianity Today*, January 21, 2011. Accessed May 18, 2017. http://www.christianitytoday.com/ct/2011/januaryweb-only/gospelstevejobs.html?start=2
[63] Jürgen Moltman, *Theology of Hope: On the Ground and the Implications of a Christian Eschatology* (Minneapolis: MN.: Fortress Press, 1993), 20.

God is the foundation of our hope and the one who gives us freedom from fear. Hope is an essential Christian virtue along with faith, and love, and they provide direction for all believers (1 Cor. 13:13). The Holy Spirit with his power is the one who directs and sustains all believers in their faith in the God of hope, "Now may the God of hope fill you with all joy and peace in believing, so that you will abound in hope by the power of the Holy Spirit" (Rom. 15:13). Hope and freedom from fear are essential elements of the Holy Spirit's role in anointed teaching.

Through the Lord Jesus Christ, God offers peace, grace, and hope (Rom. 5:1-2). The hope that God provides does not disappoint because "the love of God has been poured out within our hearts through the Holy Spirit who was given to us" (Rom. 5:5). In the Holy Spirit's power, we can face tribulations with the confidence that God will surely walk with us and ultimately will deliver us. In this way, anointed teaching includes an essential eschatological focus that brings comfort to both students and teachers. Brian Dailey's definition of eschatology is particularly helpful to understand its importance for the Christian life and anointed teaching: "Eschatology is the hope of believing people that the incompleteness of their present experience of God will be resolved, their present thirst for God fulfilled, their present need for release and salvation realized."[64] God through his Spirit sustains us as we hope in the present with complete freedom from fear.

In the Old Testament we find two examples of believers who struggled with many difficulties that entirely affected their lives and their societies. The circumstances they describe in some way are similar to the present time with our struggles, but in other ways they were even worse because they faced God's punishment for his people who violated his covenant and committed spiritual adultery.[65] As people of faith and leaders, Isaiah and Habakkuk model the circumstances and message that anointed teachers should consider in their ministries.

## Isaiah

The prophet Isaiah, whose name means, "the Lord is salvation," ministered in the Southern Kingdom of Judah after the Northern

---

[64] Brian Daley, *The Hope of the Early Church: A Handbook of Patristic Eschatology* (Grand Rapids: Baker Academic, 1991), 1.

[65] For further discussion about this topic see Raymond C. Ortlund Jr., *'God's Unfaithful Wife: A Biblical Theology of Spiritual Adultery*. New Studies in Biblical Theology 2, (Downers Grove, IL.: IVP Academic, 1996).

Kingdom of Israel had fallen to Assyria.[66] Isaiah prophesied in the reigns of Uzziah (790-739 B.C), Jotham (750-733 B.C.), Ahaz (735-715 B.C.), and Hezekiah (729-686 B.C.), all kings of Judah (1:1). The book of Isaiah has 66 chapters divided in two major sections. In this way it mirrors the Bible that has 66 books divided in two major sections, Old Testament and New Testament. In the first section, chapters 1-39, Isaiah stressed the majesty and judgment of God to Judah, surrounding nations, and all the earth. In the second section, chapters 40-66, Isaiah's focus is on God's uniqueness, eternality, and deliverance of his people.[67]

Isaiah 40 presents a vivid description about the God of hope. This chapter provides an important framework that Christian teachers can follow to understand the power of God to fulfill his promises of deliverance and to provide encouragement to God's people who face difficult circumstances in their lives. Boda explains the context for the beginning of this chapter: "The mood of the second major part of the book of Isaiah is set from the beginning of the section in Isaiah 40:1-2 where the prophet is commissioned within the heavenly council to comfort the community who endured the fulfillment of Isaiah's announcement of judgment to Hezekiah in Isaiah 39."[68] The first two verses proclaim comfort and God's deliverance:

> Comfort, comfort my people
> "Comfort, O comfort My people," says your God.
> "Speak kindly to Jerusalem;
> And call out to her, that her warfare has ended,
> That her iniquity has been removed,
> That she has received of the LORD'S hand
> Double for all her sins."

In verses 3-5 Isaiah announces that God's message transcends difficulties. Even though the present reality seems precarious, God's glory will be revealed in a way that will become evident to all. We can trust in God because he always fulfills his promises. Verses 6-11 declare that God's word is the basis of hope. People's lives and experiences are temporary, "but the word of our God stands forever" (v.8).

When we face difficulties we can rely in God's promises. However, sometimes those promises seem distant from our present realities because

---

[66] Charles Dyer and Eugene Merrill, *Old Testament Explorer: Discovering the Essence, Background, and meaning of Every Book in the Old Testament*. Swindoll Leadership Library. (Nashville, TN.: Word Publishing, 2001), 523.

[67] Dyer, 524

[68] Mark J. Boda, *'Return to Me.' A Biblical Theology of Repentance*. New Studies in Biblical Theology 35. (Downers Grove, IL.: IVP Academic, 2015), 70.

of the magnitude of our problems. The people of God at that time had lost everything; the temple had been destroyed, and they were living in exile. Isaiah reminds them that they can trust in God's word because the foundation of our hope is a God who is always able to honor his pledges regardless of the circumstances. Therefore, the remaining verses in Isaiah 40 focuses on the God who is superior to all possible oppositions.[69]

The people of God were under the dominion of the most powerful nation in the world at that time. It was natural to doubt the promise divine deliverance and in verses 12-17 Isaiah reminds them that God is superior to all human opposition because He is the creator God of the universe. There are four rhetorical questions in verses 12-14 that illustrate God's infinite wisdom and power:

> Who has measured the waters in the hollow of His hand,
> And marked off the heavens by the span,
> And calculated the dust of the earth by the measure,
> And weighed the mountains in a balance
> And the hills in a pair of scales?
> Who has directed the Spirit of the LORD,
> Or as His counselor has informed Him?
> With whom did He consult and who gave Him understanding?
> And who taught Him in the path of justice and taught Him knowledge
> And informed Him of the way of understanding?

The conclusion to these questions in verses 15-17 emphasize that there is not even a comparison between the powers of all nations combined with the powerful God. In fact, God's omnipotence and greatness make all nations less than nothing and futile:

> Behold, the nations are like a drop from a bucket,
> And are regarded as a speck of dust on the scales;
> Behold, He lifts up the islands like fine dust.
> Even Lebanon is not enough to burn,
> Nor its beasts enough for a burnt offering.
> All the nations are as nothing before Him,
> They are regarded by Him as less than nothing and meaningless.

Surrounded by polytheistic cultures, Isaiah reminds God's people in verses 18-20 that only their God is the true God. Craftsmen create all idols, but nobody can create or even make a representation of the awesome true God. Our God is superior to all spiritual opposition and we can rest and hope in him.

---

[69] The general outline of this section comes from Dyer, 563-564

To whom then will you liken God?
Or what likeness will you compare with Him?
As for the idol, a craftsman casts it,
A goldsmith plates it with gold,
And a silversmith fashions chains of silver.
He who is too impoverished for such an offering
Selects a tree that does not rot;
He seeks out for himself a skillful craftsman
To prepare an idol that will not totter.

All kings and rules of the world enjoy their authority for a short period. Even the greatest empires and political leaders vanish over time. Our God is transcendent and his dominion is incomparable. No human being or even all of them together can resist God's designs. In verses 21-24, Isaiah asks again four rhetorical questions and concludes that our confidence in God is secure because nobody can challenge his authority:

Do you not know? Have you not heard?
Has it not been declared to you from the beginning?
Have you not understood from the foundations of the earth?
It is He who sits above the circle of the earth,
And its inhabitants are like grasshoppers,
Who stretches out the heavens like a curtain
And spreads them out like a tent to dwell in.
He it is who reduces rulers to nothing,
Who makes the judges of the earth meaningless.
Scarcely have they been planted,
Scarcely have they been sown,
Scarcely has their stock taken root in the earth,
But He merely blows on them, and they wither,
And the storm carries them away like stubble.

When we face difficulties, we have a tendency to oftentimes see our problems as too big to be solved. In these circumstances we need get the appropriate perspective of our situation in comparison with the vastness of our world. As we look at the stars at night we can easily realize how small we really are. Isaiah reminds us in verses 25-26 that the God of the universe not only created all stars, but he calls them by name. We can have freedom from fear when we rest in God's greatness and might.

"To whom then will you liken Me
That I would be his equal?" says the Holy One.

Lift up your eyes on high
And see who has created these stars,
The One who leads forth their host by number,
He calls them all by name;
Because of the greatness of His might and the strength of His power,
Not one of them is missing.

Our God is both powerful and approachable. He is omniscient, eternal, and omnipotent and yet he is a personal God who knows our needs and cares for us. Israel doubted God's concern for their problems and Isaiah states in verses 27-28 that even though we may question or doubt God, he is permanently present with us and always cares for our needs.

Why do you say, O Jacob, and assert, O Israel,
"My way is hidden from the LORD,
And the justice due me escapes the notice of my God"?
God's questions: Do you not know? Have you not heard?
God's answers: The Everlasting God, the LORD, the Creator of the ends
of the earth. Does not become weary or tired. His understanding is
inscrutable.

The conclusion of this chapter in verses 29-31 gives an application that believers can apply in times of problems and tribulations. God gives strength to those who trust in him. The God of hope sustains us in all circumstances. When we focus only in our problems it becomes natural to get discouraged, but when our primary focus is on the Lord, we become free from fear as we wait for him:

He gives strength to the weary,
And to him who lacks might He increases power.
Though youths grow weary and tired,
And vigorous young men stumble badly,
Yet those who wait for the LORD
Will gain new strength;
They will mount up with wings like eagles,
They will run and not get tired,
They will walk and not become weary.

Isaiah 40 reminds us that we can trust in God's promises and in the God of hope who always fulfills his promises. The unrivaled sovereignty of the Creator God is a key theme in Isaiah.[70] Nowadays, the Holy Spirit sustains us and liberates us from fear in an uncertain world as we rest with confidence in the God of hope. In the Old Testament we find another example that guides us in our trust in God in times of difficulties.

## Habakkuk

The Old Testament prophet Habakkuk teaches us that God is always in control in spite of how our present circumstances may look like. We can rest in God's sovereignty that gives us freedom of fear even in the middle of his punishment. We can hope in the God of the universe and we can then bring encouragement to our students in our teaching ministries.

Habakkuk was a prophet in Judea, the southern kingdom, after the fall of Nineveh in 612 B.C. before the first Babylonian invasion of Judea in August 605 B.C. It was a time of tyranny and social chaos; people were oppressed; God's people sinned openly and idolatry was extensively practiced.[71]

The book of Habakkuk has three chapters and presents a simple structure. Habakkuk begins this short book with a complain; God answers. Habakkuk complains again and God responds to his objection. The book ends with a psalm of praise that beautifully describes Habakkuk's commitment to continue trusting in the Lord who is in complete control of everything.

The first four verses of chapter one portray the first protest of Habakkuk against God. In fact, the word prophecy at the beginning of the book can be translated as "burden." Habakkuk faces a crisis of faith because he cannot understand why God does not act against the evil of his people as he has clearly promised to do. Habakkuk knows that the Holy God does not tolerate sin. However, God's people sinned without control and apparently God was not fulfilling his promises. Amid these circumstances, Habakkuk cries and asks God, "How long, O Lord will I call for help and you will not hear?" (v. 2). In this question, Habakkuk resembles all of us who have a tendency to question God's wisdom when our theology does not seem to match with our reality.

God responds to Habakkuk in verses 1:5-11. He is not indifferent; in fact, he is already acting to discipline his people for their wicked deeds. God was preparing the Chaldeans to punish Judah's sins. The Chaldeans

---

[70] Richard L. Schultz, "Isaiah, Book of" in Kevin J. Vanhoozer (Ed.) *Dictionary for Theological Interpretation of the Bible*. (Grand Rapids, MI.: Baker Academic, 2005), 340.
[71] My article "Dios está en Control" in the Talbot Good Book Blog deals with many of the ideas for the Habakkuk section https://www.biola.edu/blogs/good-book-blog/2013/dios-esta-en-control

were the Babylonian Empire established by King Nabopolassar and magnified by Nebuchadnezzar. The Babylonians were a powerful nation known for its cruelty. God always acts even though we might have the impression that he is silent or indifferent.

Nevertheless, for Habakkuk the solution seems worse that the problem. How is it possible that God would use a vile and evil nation to discipline his own people? Starting in verse 1:12 Habakkuk struggles with the apparent inconsistency between his theology and his present experience. Habakkuk does not understand God's purposes. We all can appreciate his honesty and many times identify with his feelings. However, in spite of his internal conflict to comprehend God's will, Habakkuk patiently awaits in the divine answer (2:1). God is omniscient and in difficult times the best thing we can do is to seek his face and trust him. We can rest in his perfect will even when we fail to understand it or even question his timing.

God graciously answers again Habakkuk question in verses 2-20 of Chapter 2. God asks that a messenger read the vision and run to spread the news. The divine plans will be fulfilled even if it seems that they are delayed. Therefore, verse four summarizes the appropriate way in which we can relate to God, "but the righteous will live by his faith." Without faith it is impossible to please God (Heb. 11:1). Faith in the mighty and loving God of the universe sustains us in times of fear and difficulties.

God always keeps his promises to punish evil and injustice. The expression "woe" indicates condemnation and punishment for opposing God and his ways. God pronounces five woes specifically against the Chaldeans, but in general against those who oppose him rejecting his ways:

1. Woe against those who by intimidation and force take what is no theirs (2:6-8).
2. Woe against those who find its security only on physical places (2:9-11).
3. Woe against those who practice tyranny and oppression (2:12-13).
4. Woe against opportunists (2:15-17).
5. Woe against idolaters (2:18-19).

Within these expressions of judgment, God gives two promises: the earth will be filled with the knowledge of the fear of the Lord (v.14), and the Lord is in his holy temple (v. 20). God is in control in spite of our doubts, fears, and insecurities. Since God is sovereign over all creation, the earth must remain silent in his presence. God reminds Habakkuk that he is in charge of what happens and that his plans ultimately will be successful. Habakkuk "learned that he must continue to believe and trust in the promises of the Lord despite what he might encounter in his own circumstances and situations."[72] Therefore, like Habakkuk, we enjoy freedom from fear, as we trust him.

The book of Habakkuk concludes with a prayer of praise to the God who can be trusted completely. Chapter three is a psalm that exalts the majesty of God (3-15) and the confidence that human beings can have on his majesty (16-19). Habakkuk "could rejoice in God even in time of hardship and difficulty because God would supply the strength and stability needed to endure the uncertain days ahead."[73] We also with Habakkuk can rest in the God who saves, and serves as our refuge. In a climate of fear and despair, we rest in the God who has absolute control over all circumstances. We can trust completely in our Lord.

## The Holy Spirit that Liberates Us from Fear

In Jesus Christ, our relationship with God the Father through the Holy Spirit becomes intimate and personal. In Christ and with the Holy Spirit's leading, we enjoy the privilege of being children of God. The apostle Paul eloquently describes this important reality in Romans 8:12-17:

> So then, brethren, we are under obligation, not to the flesh, to live according to the flesh—for if you are living according to the flesh, you must die; but if by the Spirit you are putting to death the deeds of the body, you will live. For all who are being led by the Spirit of God, these are sons of God. For you have not received a spirit of slavery leading to fear again, but you have received a spirit of adoption as sons by which we cry out, "Abba! Father!" The Spirit Himself testifies with our spirit that we are children of God, and if children, heirs also, heirs of God and fellow heirs with Christ, if indeed we suffer with *Him* so that we may also be glorified with *Him*.

As children of God we are free from fear. The Spirit in us confirms that we are loved, accepted, and protected by the Father. As a father myself, I am committed to always care for my children. I honor this commitment because of my deep love for them, not for any external pressure or a feeling of obligation. My children know that I love them and that I will do anything for their well-being. The God of the universe is our heavenly Father and not only he is the sovereign Lord of the

---

[72] Eugene H. Merrill, Mark F. Rooker, and Michael A. Grisanti, *The World and the Word: An Introduction to the Old Testament*, (Nashville, TN.: B&H Academic, 2011), 470.
[73] Dyer, 806

universe, but he also loves us as his children. Anointed teaching centers in the acknowledgment and proclamation of this important truth that completely shapes how live our lives in the middle of uncertain times.

The Holy Spirit gives us freedom from fear not only from external circumstances, but also from our own insecurities. The monumental task to represent Christ can be daunting for teachers who are responsible for the students under their wings. Timothy was a young leader with an important ministry and the apostle Paul encouraged him with the following words, "for this reason I remind you to kindle afresh the gift of God which is in you through the laying on of my hands. For God has not given us a spirit of timidity, but of power and love and discipline" (2 Tim. 1: 6-7). The Holy Spirit empowers us to boldly serve the Lord with confidence.

Life is tough and these are difficult times. Christian teachers and their students are not immune from these circumstances. However, instead of living with fear as most people do, we enjoy the Holy Spirit's freedom from fear as we wait and trust in the God of hope who always cares for us. Anointed teaching brings the Holy Spirit's comfort to everybody who is willing to have faith in the sovereign God.

# PART TWO

# Teaching in the Spirit and Celebration

In considering of the themes of Moses' Song, Hannah's Prayer and Mary's Magnificat, we propose anointed Christian teaching that celebrates, also incarnates five freedoms for living today in the third millennium. We seek to incarnate freedom for truth, freedom for love, freedom for faith, freedom for hope and freedom for joy in our Christian teaching, learning and living. Second Corinthians 3:6 makes this clear where the Apostle Paul notes "God has us competent to be ministers of a new covenant, not of the letter but of the spirit; for the letter kills, but the Spirit gives life." In the contemporary incarnation of our lives, we celebrate those Christian virtues that Jesus calls us to replicate in our teaching ministries. The Christian Church celebrates freedom for truth, love, faith, hope and joy in its Christian education ministries. Teaching in the name, spirit and power of Jesus calls us to such a mission. This is our Eucharistic calling and identity that serves to distinguish Christian teaching and learning in the world of educational theory and practice.

What five virtues are celebrated in anointed Christian teaching that builds upon the spiritual and whole-life liberation we experience in Jesus Christ? The virtues identified above, namely truth, love, faith, hope and joy serve to connect teaching ministries to biblical sources that identify the perennial purposes of the Christian church. These purposes are proclamation, fellowship/community formation, service, advocacy and worship. For these purposes to be fulfilled, the gifts and enablement of the Holy Spirit who works in partnership with Christian believers is indispensable. Christian teachers and learners are called to celebrate and rely upon the Spirit in order to proclaim truth, to nurture love in community, to serve faithfully, to advocate with a sense of hope, and to worship joyfully in the everyday tasks of teaching and learning. These are ideals that are worth our best educational efforts in partnership with the Holy Spirit.

To draw upon a culinary metaphor, the five virtues are the dishes set upon the table of educational offerings for all to enjoy. One definition for teaching is the artful setting of an inviting table that welcomes all to participate and results in joyful celebration.[74] The complement to the celebration is the place of lament where God's purposes and desires are compared with human realities which call for the liberation noted in Part One of this work and reconsidered in Part Three where the challenge of sustenance emerges as Christians await the full salvation of all of creation made possible at the second coming of Christ.

Biblical passages that describe the table God sets for teachers and students alike include Proverbs 9:1-6 where Wisdom's Feast is beautifully described and invites all to partake in gaining maturity, living and walking in the way of insight. This is what teachers hope for in their curricular offerings. Isaiah 55:1-3a extends yet another invitation for believers:

> Ho, everyone who thirsts, come to the waters;
> And you that have no money, come, buy and eat!
> Come, buy wine and milk without money and without price.
> Why do you spend your money for that which is not bread,
> And labor for that which does not satisfy?
> Listen carefully to me, and eat what is good,
> And delight yourselves in rich food.
> Incline your ear, and come to me;
> Listen, so that you may live.

Jesus himself is the host who offers nourishment and life to all who partake, fulfilling the promise of Isaiah 55. As Christian teachers participate in the table fellowship made possible by the Holy Spirit, their teaching impacts the hearts, minds and spirits of learners. The Last Supper that Jesus celebrated with his disciples is instituted as a continuing meal that the Christian community embraces (1 Cor 11:23-12:11). Through its participation, the Christian Church lives out its Eucharistic identity that is suggested in John's account of Jesus' post-resurrection appearance by the Sea of Galilee. Having visited Israel and the shore of the Sea of Galilee for the first time in January 2016 where I had a meal of Saint Peter's fish in Tiberias, this text assumes a vivid connection in my recent memory. In this appearance Jesus prepares a meal and after confronting Peter, he issues a three-fold command to feed and tend his lambs and sheep in following him that has implications for anointed teaching:

---

[74] Robert W. Pazmiño, *Basics of Teaching for Christians* (Grand Rapids: Baker Books, 1998), 11.

After these things Jesus showed himself again to the disciples by the Sea of Tiberias; and he showed himself in this way. Gathered there together were Simon Peter, Thomas called the Twin, Nathanael of Cana in Galilee, the sons of Zebedee, and two others of his disciples. Simon Peter said to them, "I am going fishing." They said to him, "We will go with you." They went out and got into the boat, but that night they caught nothing. Just after daybreak, Jesus stood on the beach; but the disciples did not know that it was Jesus. Jesus said to them, "Children, you have no fish, have you?" They answered him, "No." He said to them, "Cast the net to the right side of the boat, and you will find some." So they cast it, and now they were not able to haul it in because there were so many fish. That disciple whom Jesus loved said to Peter, "It is the Lord!" When Simon Peter heard that it was the Lord, he put on some clothes, for he was naked, and jumped into the sea. But the other disciples came in the boat, dragging the net full of fish, for they were not far from the land, only about a hundred yards off. When they had gone ashore, they saw a charcoal fire there, with fish on it, and bread. Jesus said to them, "Bring some of the fish that you have just caught." So Simon Peter went aboard and hauled the net ashore, full of large fish, a hundred fifty-three of them; and though there were so many, the net was not torn. Jesus said to them, "Come and have breakfast." Now none of the disciples dared to ask him, "Who are you?" because they knew it was the Lord. Jesus came and took the bread and gave it to them, and did the same with the fish. This was now the third time that Jesus appeared to the disciples after he was raised from the dead. When they had finished breakfast, Jesus said to Simon Peter, "Simon son of John, do you love me more than these?" He said to him, "Yes, Lord; you know that I love you." Jesus said to him, "Feed my lambs." A second time he said to him, "Simon son of John, do you love me?" He said to him, "Yes, Lord; you know that I love you." Jesus said to him, "Tend my sheep." He said to him the third time, "Simon son of John, do you love me?" Peter felt hurt because he said to him the third time, "Do you love me?" And he said to him, "Lord, you know everything; you know that I love you." Jesus said to him, "Feed my sheep. Very truly, I tell you, when you were younger, you used to fasten your own belt and to go wherever you wished. But when you grow old, you will stretch out your hands, and someone else will fasten a belt around you and take you where you do not wish to go." (He said this to indicate the kind of death by which he would glorify God.) After this he said to him, "Follow me" (John 21:1-19).

Following after Jesus in a teaching ministry requires reliance upon the Spirit to serve at the metaphorical table those virtues capable of forming the character and life of students in fulfilling Jesus' command to Peter and all his disciples to feed and tend his lambs and sheep. Teaching is a ministry for nurturing and feeding children, youth and adults primarily at the intellectual level, but also embracing the emotional, social, moral, physical and spiritual dimensions of persons because feeding and tending requires a holistic approach to life.

Ted Ward provides a helpful hand model for envisioning these six dimensions of persons in relationship to teaching.[75] Each of these dimensions can be primarily related to five Christian virtues for each of the five fingers, with the palm of the hand being the spiritual dimension that links each of the distinct fingers named below. The following pairings are possible for each of the fingers:

- Faith-physical (thumb)
- Truth-intellectual (pointer)
- Joy-emotional (middle finger)
- Love-social (ring finger)
- Hope-moral (pinkie)

The palm is the spiritual and relational link that serves to connect all of these dimensions to see persons in the ministries of teaching and learning as whole and holy while being embraced by the Holy Spirit to become all that God intends. This was Jesus' intent as he encountered Peter on the shore of the Sea of Tiberias after his denial, and commanded him to feed and tend his lambs and sheep. On that recent trip to Israel and the region of Galilee, I along with ten students in the city of Tiberias had lunch at a restaurant located right over the shore of the Sea of Galilee as we enjoyed St. Peter fish from the menu on a sunny winter day with sixty degree weather. On that occasion I recalled Jesus' restoring and teaching of Peter as I sought to teach my students about celebrating our Christian faith while on our pilgrimage that explored religious education in Israel.

---

[75] Ted Ward, *Values Begin at Home*, 2nd. ed. (Wheaton, Ill.: Victor, 1989), 18.

CHAPTER SIX

# Teaching and Freedom for Truth
Octavio J. Esqueda

*The way to right wrongs is to turn the light of truth upon them.*
*Ida B. Wells*

*When the Helper comes, whom I will send to you from the Father, that*
*is the Spirit of truth who proceeds from the Father, He will testify about*
*Me, and you will testify also, because you have been with Me from the*
*beginning. John 15:26-27*

Truth is an essential pillar of any society. A community can only
successfully work when relationships have truth as a key foundation. For
this reason, in the United States during lawsuits witnesses are required to
solemnly to affirm the following words at the beginning of their
testimonies, "Do you swear to tell the truth, the whole truth, and nothing
but the truth." There cannot be real justice nor establish long lasting
relationships with falsehoods and lies. In the same way, Christianity and
teaching anointed with the Holy Spirit have truth as a core element for
their message and practice.

Truth is the foundation for the good news of the Gospel of Christ to
the world. When the religious leaders brought Jesus to Pontius Pilate, the
governor of Judea, to be judged and condemned to die on the cross, Jesus
defined his purpose and identity when he was asked if he was the king of
the Jews with the following words, "You say *correctly* that I am a king.
For this I have been born, and for this I have come into the world, to
testify to the truth. Everyone who is of the truth hears My voice" (John
18:37). When he heard this astonishing response, Pilate then asked one of
humanity's essential inquiries, "What is truth?" (John 18:38). The answer
we give to this question defines our worldview and the way we live.
Furthermore, our answer to this question also shapes our faith and
teaching. For Christians, truth goes beyond merely stating correct
assertions. Truth is personal. The triune God *is* truth.

For this reason, the Christian faith and followers of Christ are
established in the God of truth. Teaching with the Holy Spirit's anointing

gives freedom to become messengers of truth to everybody around us.[76] The truth from God teaches us, reproofs us, corrects us, and trains us in divine righteousness (2 Tim. 3:16).

## God Is Truth

Truth is one of God's essential attributes. As such, this attribute does not merely mean that God is truthful or that his claims coincide with reality, but that the triune God is the Truth. The three persons in the Trinity are truth at all times without any falsehood in them. The God of the Bible is faithful to his promises and we can always trust him. The Word of God affirms that every person in the Trinity possesses truth as part of their divine essence.

God the Father is the truth. Deuteronomy 32:4 describes the character of the righteous God we can proclaim and praise with complete confidence, "*He is* the Rock, His work *is* perfect; For all His ways *are* justice, A God of truth and without injustice; Righteous and upright *is* He" (NKJV). God is our rock and at all times and during all circumstances we can rest in his promises. God's faithfulness is great and his loyal love is forever. For this reason, when we teach others about our God's character and love for everybody we provide refreshment and peace: "Let my teaching drop as the rain, My speech distill as the dew, As the droplets on the fresh grass And as the showers on the herb" (Dt. 32:2). Our words and teaching bring freedom when they are based on the God of truth (Is. 65:16).

Jesus Christ is the truth. Our Lord Jesus Christ is the foundation of our faith. In John 14:6, Jesus made an important claim that describes his personality and his purpose when he came into this world: "Jesus said to him, I am the way, and the truth, and the life; no one comes to the Father but through Me." Jesus Christ is the only mediator between God and all human beings (1 Tim. 2:5). Only in in the Son of God we can receive life, not only eternal life, but also the fulness of life (John 3:16; John 10:10; 1 John 5:12). Jesus is the way to the Father, the source of life, and also the truth. Jesus no only speaks truth, but with the Father and the Holy Spirit he is the truth.

The Holy Spirit just like the other members of the Godhead is the truth. In John 14:16-17, Jesus promised to his disciples, and to all of us, that the Holy Spirit would live and dwell in all of his followers: "I will ask the Father, and He will give you another Helper, that He may be with you forever; *that is* the Spirit of truth, whom the world cannot receive,

---

[76] Octavio J. Esqueda, "The Holy Spirit as Teacher" in *The Teaching Ministry of the Church*, 2nd edition. (Nashville: B&H Academic, 2008), 78.

because it does not see Him or know Him, *but* you know Him because He abides with you and will be in you." The Holy Spirit lives with us as our counselor-helper-advocate (*paraklete*) and has the same divine essence as Christ. The Holy Spirit, just like the father and the Son is the Spirit of truth.

Since the three persons of the Trinity not only speak the truth, but are the truth, everything that flows from them is always truthful. Therefore, the Word of God is truth and sanctifies us (John 17:17-19). God's message always has truth as the foundation and Christian teachers are heralds of truth to a world that just as Pontius Pilate continuously is asking "what is truth?"

In fact, human beings are inclined to constantly lie. The *Dr. House* was a popular television show in the United States; Dr. House was a medical doctor and one of his distinctive catching phrases was "everybody lies." The Psalmist in Psalm 12:1-2 acknowledges this situation with the following lamentation, "Help, LORD, for the godly man ceases to be, For the faithful disappear from among the sons of men. They speak falsehood to one another; With flattering lips and with a double heart they speak." The Bible clearly commands us to set aside falsehood and lies (Ex. 20:16) and yet all of us frequently break this commandment and sin. Surely it seems that a delight for falsehood is the natural disposition of all human beings (Ps. 62:4).

Nevertheless, the new life that Jesus offers through his sacrifice at the cross transforms our lives completely. In Christ, our new identity is now established in the God of truth. Therefore, we now have the calling to set aside lies and to live in the sanctity of truth:

> But you did not learn Christ in this way, if indeed you have heard Him and have been taught in Him, just as truth is in Jesus, that, in reference to your former manner of life, you lay aside the old self, which is being corrupted in accordance with the lusts of deceit, and that you be renewed in the spirit of your mind, and put on the new self, which in *the likeness of* God has been created in righteousness and holiness of the truth. Therefore, laying aside falsehood, SPEAK TRUTH EACH ONE *of you* WITH HIS NEIGHBOR, for we are members of one another. (Eph. 4:20-25)

An essential characteristic of the Christian faith and anointed teaching is to always speak with the truth. As children of God we all have the Holy Spirit anointing and we are members of one another in Christ's body. Lying and falsehood have no place in the Church and even less in those who have the privilege of teach others about God. We all need each other and nobody has complete exclusivity of God's message.

For this reason, the ability to recognize our ignorance about some issues, our complete dependence on divine wisdom, and our need for others to better understand God are fundamental elements of teaching with the anointing of the Spirit.

## Our Limitations

The sovereign God of the universe is always truthful and loves truth (Ps. 51:6). However, even though we were created in God's image, we are finite and imperfect. As Christians, and especially as Christian educators we need to recognize our limitations and to never believe that we are the sole owners of truth. Sadly, it becomes very common to follow extreme positions like a pendulum that leads us to either believe that Christian orthodoxy must agree with our ideas and preferences or to believe that nobody can affirm with certainty any doctrine because they depend on general consensus or personal interpretation. Both positions find their basis on pride that makes humans the judges of God's message. We can know God and proclaim with confidence his ways, but at the same time we can admit that our knowledge of God is limited and that the Holy Spirit also speaks to other people although their perspectives differ from ours.

The Bible illustrates this apparent tension between the possibility we have to know God and the impossibility of fully comprehend him. Jeremiah 9:23-24 sates the following:

> Thus says the LORD, Let not a wise man boast of his wisdom, and let not the mighty man boast of his might, let not a rich man boast of his riches; but let him who boasts boast of this, that he understands and knows Me, that I am the LORD who exercises lovingkindness, justice and righteousness on earth; for I delight in these things, declares the LORD.

This passage teaches us that it is possible and even desirable to know and understand God. In fact, this knowledge is practical because it leads us to value what God values and to imitate him. Theology, the knowledge of God, always has practical implications and should result in a life that pursues mercy and righteousness. This practical theology should be the most important priority of our lives and the only activity that bring meaning to our lives.

Nonetheless, Isaiah 55:8-9 reminds us that even though we can know God, our perspective is always limited to understand the majestic and omniscience of the sovereign God of the universe:

"For My thoughts are not your thoughts,
Nor are your ways My ways," declares the LORD.
"For *as* the heavens are higher than the earth,
So are My ways higher than your ways
And My thoughts than your thoughts.

God knows everything and he always speak the truth, but we are imperfect. We can never be like God. Our limitations demonstrate our great need and dependence on the Lord. We need him and we need others in our lives to help us refine our thinking.

I have frequently heard many believers say that when they see God face to face they would be able to understand why God decided to act in certain ways that they cannot comprehend at the present time. They believe that one day they will fully grasp God's plans. The reality, however, is that we will never be able to fully understand God. Every day we can grow in our knowledge of God and one day we will be with him for all eternity, but God will continue being majestic and we will remain his creatures. An eternity will not be enough to stop glorifying our amazing God.

## God Is the Source of Wisdom

The God of truth is al so the source of true wisdom. Our limitations prevent us to fully understand our reality; God not only knows everything, but he desires to teach us his ways. For this reason, the Bible declares emphatically that the beginning of wisdom is the fear of the Lord (Prov. 1:7). The fear of the Lord means to live aware of who God is and who we are. The wisdom and knowledge of God are so majestic that not even all the knowledge we could acquire during our lives would compare to it (Rom. 11:33).

Several years ago, when I was a seminary student in Dallas somebody gave an advice that I have not forgotten and that I value more as time goes by because of its simplicity and depth. These are the wise words of advice I received: "remember that there is but one God, and you are not him." This is a fundamental principle for seminary students and for all in the Christian life. Afterwards, I heard the same idea expressed in a different way, "there are no openings in the Trinity!" We need to remember that our lives completely depend on divine providence. The freedom for truth that God gives us through the Holy Spirit depends only in his grace and not on ourselves. Only the triune God is our Teacher and the only one who deserves our complete admiration and devotion.

Consequently, not a single leader o Christian teacher can occupy God's place as the one who dictates the regulations people need to follow. We are God's messengers, but we lack the divine authority to judge others. When we confuse our voice and teaching with God's voice, we place ourselves as God and become idolaters and distort authentic anointed teaching. We commit a huge heresy when we confuse our opinions and perspectives with the central tenants of the Christian faith. This situation becomes possible when we believe we are the only recipients of divine wisdom and that people with other perspectives are wrong. Sadly, this is a very common attitude among many pastors and Christian leaders who believe their main divine calling is fighting to protect what they believe is the purity of the biblical message at all cost. They fail to realize that when they equate their opinions with God's truths they do exactly the opposite to what they teach and preach. Indeed, humility is an essential characteristic of anointed teaching.

We all need the Holy Spirit direction and illumination in our lives. Only the Spirit of God understand fully the God of truth.[77] Through the ministry of the Holy Spirit God reveals to us the things he has prepared for us. We can only know God's truths through the Holy Spirit as 1 Corinthians 2:9-13 clearly explains:

> But just as it is written,
> "THINGS WHICH EYE HAS NOT SEEN AND EAR HAS NOT HEARD,
> AND *which* HAVE NOT ENTERED THE HEART OF MAN,
> ALL THAT GOD HAS PREPARED FOR THOSE WHO LOVE HIM."
> For to us God revealed *them* through the Spirit; for the Spirit searches
> all things, even the depths of God. For who among men knows the
> *thoughts* of a man except the spirit of the man which is in him? Even so
> the *thoughts* of God no one knows except the Spirit of God. Now we
> have received, not the spirit of the world, but the Spirit who is from
> God, so that we may know the things freely given to us by God, which
> things we also speak, not in words taught by human wisdom, but in
> those taught by the Spirit, combining spiritual *thoughts* with spiritual
> *words*.

The Holy Spirit teaches us God's ways. Real wisdom comes from God who invites us to depend on him so we can live and teach with integrity (Jam. 1:5). Therefore, in the Christian life, a complete dependence on the Holy Spirit is an indispensable requirement. A life of prayer is key to receive God's message and then to share it with others. Nonetheless, we need to remember that God's message is not restricted to only a few people, but it is a divine gift of grace for everybody.

---

[77] Ibid., p. 79

## The Importance of Community

The God of truth desires to reveal himself to all people and nobody has exclusive rights of God's message. For this reason, Christian teaching and wisdom always take place in the context of community. Our assumptions always affect the way we see life and interpret our circumstances. We all have prejudices and our life outlook is partial and limited. However, we can find comfort in the good news that we are not on our own because the solution to our myopia is always found in community. Listening to the perspectives and opinions of others helps us to better understand our reality. For this reason, humility is the first step towards true wisdom and the worst case of ignorance is when we don't know that we don't know, but we think we know. Only when are aware of our deep need for others we can expand our knowledge to see life with more clarity.

Consequently, the Christian life and Bible teaching must take place in community where all believers have the opportunity to express their voices. We can only interpret the Scriptures correctly in community under the Holy Spirit's direction. In the same way, besides the the need for multicultural perspectives, we also must listen to women's perspectives about biblical interpretation. With frequency, biblical narratives are taught from the perspective of men and, in this way, our interpretation could be distorted in some cases even though it represents the one usually accepted.

For example, the book *Vindicating the Vixens: Revisiting Sexualized, Vilified, and Marginalized Women of the Bible*[78] has helped me to better understand several biblical stories that I already knew, but did not realize that were interpreted incorrectly. but that traditionally have been interpreted in a wrong way. The principles of biblical hermeneutics have not changed, but our perspective was limited because we did not have the perspective of other people, especially women, when we read the biblical stories. I had lost the richness and significance about the stories of many women in the Bible because I had not seen key elements in the narrative even though they were always there.

When we are humble and we obey the biblical exhortation of "teaching and admonishing one another" (Col. 3:16) our understanding expands and our perspective about reality gets enlighten. There is nothing worse than prideful believers who think they know everything. We enrich our lives when we walk together and learn from each under the Holy Spirit's guidance. Without a doubt we need everybody and

---

[78] Sandra Glahn (ed.). *Vindicating the Vixens: Revisiting Sexualized, Vilified, and Marginalized Women of the Bible* (Grand Rapids: Kregel, 2017).

when we listen and value all voices we all learn better, see better, and walk in this life in a better way.

## Conclusion

The Holy Spirit's presence in our lives radically transforms our lives in a way that produces the fruit of celebration and through his anointing it gives us the freedom to live and proclaim God's truth. Anointed teaching convicts the world of sin, righteousness, and judgement and at the same time brings glory to God. Jesus promised that the coming of the Holy Spirit would change will completely change the life of his disciples. In fact, Jesus told us that it would be better for us that he leaves because the Holy Spirit now lives in us forever. The Holy Spirit's dwelling in us is the best gift that we could receive and it is the fountain of life and Christian teaching.

> But I tell you the truth, it is to your advantage that I go away; for if I do not go away, the Helper will not come to you; but if I go, I will send Him to you. And He, when He comes, will convict the world concerning sin and righteousness and judgment; concerning sin, because they do not believe in Me; and concerning righteousness, because I go to the Father and you no longer see Me; and concerning judgment, because the ruler of this world has been judged.
> "I have many more things to say to you, but you cannot bear *them* now. But when He, the Spirit of truth, comes, He will guide you into all the truth; for He will not speak on His own initiative, but whatever He hears, He will speak; and He will disclose to you what is to come. He will glorify Me, for He will take of Mine and will disclose *it* to you. All things that the Father has are Mine; therefore I said that He takes of Mine and will disclose *it* to you. (John 16:7-15)

CHAPTER 7

# Teaching and Freedom for Love
Robert W. Pazmiño

In 1956 when H. Richard Niebuhr considered the purpose of education, he proposed that it should nurture the love of God and neighbor reflecting Jesus' two great commandments.[79] I think that Niebuhr's purposes should now be expanded to include God's love and our love of the world (John 3:16), with the world understood as God's creation as explored theologically in chapter one. This additional purpose is crucial with the global ecological crisis that confronts humanity with all of creation groaning awaiting the full salvation God intends (Romans 8:18-30). Ideally, Christian teaching should assure the freedom for love as experienced by all participants in the hope of nurturing the love of God, neighbor, self and creation as perennial purposes worthy of attention and highest priority. But how can teaching contribute to such love and encourage students to embrace and practice such love in their daily lives? The task seems overwhelming, if not impossible.

The Apostle Paul's insights on believers' justification by faith, in Romans 5:1-5 offer some hope for Christians who teach in relation to the Christian virtue of love:

> Therefore, since we are justified by faith, we have peace with God through our Lord Jesus Christ, through whom we have obtained access to this grace in which we stand; and we boast in our hope of sharing the glory of God. And not only that, but we also boast in our sufferings, knowing that suffering produces endurance, and endurance produces character, and character produces hope, and hope does not disappoint us, because God's love has been poured into our hearts through the Holy Spirit that has been given to us.

"God's love poured into our hearts through the Holy Spirit." Christian teachers have a faith that gifts us with peace with God and God's grace for everyday living. God accompanies us in the person and

---

[79] H. Richard Niebuhr, Daniel D. Williams, and James M. Gustafson, *The Purpose of the Church and Its Ministry* (New York: Harper & Bros., 1956).

work of the Holy Spirit who is given to us as an inheritance, a legacy throughout our life journey. God's love is poured into our hearts through the Holy Spirit and it is God's love as experienced by students through the ministry of teaching that excites and motivates the love of students themselves. This requires the work of the Spirit in the hearts and spirits of students who themselves are responsible before God for their lives and commitments. Prayer is essential prior to, during and after any teaching encounter for the Spirit to have freedom to work with both teachers and students alike. Active listening to the Spirit's redirection even in the midst of instruction is important when we assume the presence of God's Spirit in all that transpires in a teaching ministry.

Paul in his second letter to Timothy describes his love and concern for Timothy whom he mentored in the faith in the following passage:

> I am grateful to God—whom I worship with a clear conscience, as my ancestors did—when I remember you constantly in my prayers night and day. Recalling your tears, I long to see you so that I may be filled with joy. I am reminded of your sincere faith, a faith that lived first in your grandmother Lois and your mother Eunice and now, I am sure, lives in you. For this reason I remind you to rekindle the gift of God that is within you through the laying on of my hands; for God did not give us a spirit of cowardice, but rather a spirit of power and of love and of self-discipline. (2 Tim 1:3-7)

Timothy is reminded of the spirit of love he has received to guide his ministry efforts. Reliance upon this spirit was to bear fruits in his teaching as Paul suggests a faithful progression: "and what you have heard from me through many witnesses entrust to faithful people who will be able to teach others as well" (2 Tim 2:2). The progression of faith and love was first experienced through the teaching ministry of Lois, Timothy's grandmother, and Eunice, Timothy's mother. It was continued in Paul's teaching ministry, and now was to continue in Timothy's teaching of others who in turn would also teach. All the teaching was undergirded by the spirit of love gifted to Christians and nurtured across the generations in families, faith communities, and mentoring relationships through the ministry of the Holy Spirit. God's love poured upon creation and incarnated in Jesus Christ is now extended to human kind through the Spirit's ministry.

The First Letter of John makes further explicit the connection between God's love and the love Christian teachers are able and commanded to share with our students:

Beloved, let us love one another, because love is from God; everyone who loves is born of God and knows God. Whoever does not love does not know God, for God is love. God's love was revealed among us in this way: God sent his only Son into the world so that we might live through him. In this is love, not that we loved God but that he loved us and sent his Son to be the atoning sacrifice for our sins. Beloved, since God loved us so much, we also ought to love one another. No one has ever seen God; if we love one another, God lives in us, and his love is perfected in us. (1 John 4:7-12)

The Holy Spirit is able to perfect God's love within us as a source to share with others. Being fully embraced by God's unconditional love in Jesus Christ, Christian teachers are able to share this love with their students through the presence and power of the Holy Spirit.

Earlier in that same letter, the author of First John describes the message to love one another that I think certainly applies to Christian teachers today:

For this is the message you have heard from the beginning, that we should love one another. We must not be like Cain who was from the evil one and murdered his brother. And why did he murder him? Because his own deeds were evil and his brother's righteous. Do not be astonished, brothers and sisters, that the world hates you. We know that we have passed from death to life because we love one another. Whoever does not love abides in death. All who hate a brother or sister are murderers, and you know that murderers do not have eternal life abiding in them. We know love by this, that he laid down his life for us—and we ought to lay down our lives for one another. How does God's love abide in anyone who has the world's goods and sees a brother or sister in need and yet refuses help? (1 John 3:11-17)

God's love abides in those who lay down their lives for others and share both their wisdom and goods with persons in need. Teaching is a form of laying down our lives in service for others. Teaching is a form of help responding to the need for truth, knowledge and wisdom to live this life. The realities of death also emerge in teaching with the obligation in teaching of destroying the destroyers of life with which our students contend on a daily basis. Spiritual discernment is required to engage this dimension of prophetic teaching or subversive teaching that names all that oppresses persons and offers the alternatives God intends for humanity and all of creation. This too is a loving response as well as the affirmation of the worth and dignity of each person one teaches. In this work teachers care enough and be must be willing enough to confront the various destroyers on personal, communal and corporate life that are legion in the human journey resulting in suffering, pain and oppression in various forms.

## Four Forms of Human Love: Making Distinctions

Christians have historically discussed the forms of love being *eros, philia, caritas* and *agape.*[80] A discussion of these four serves to indicate the limits of human freedom in relation to love within teaching ministries. Too many cases in the public arena have been disclosed where teachers have violated their trust with students and have even engaged in inappropriate erotic relationships. I was one of three faculty members who reviewed the case of a married faculty colleague who had unprofessional, immoral and unethical relationships with married and unmarried students. This was a clear case of boundary crossing and a misguided freedom that distorted the teaching relationship with disastrous results. Freedom needs to be balanced with the place of order and proper limits for the expression of erotic love that Christians have taught should be kept within the sacred bounds of marriage.[81] There are cases where single teachers may eventually develop amorous relationships with former single students, but the power differential between teachers and students can too easily lead to abuse and unethical boundary crossing in ministries of learning together.

In relation to *philia*, the matter of friendships between teachers and students can present a dilemma. The care of students may extend to interpersonal interactions outside of the classroom within and beyond an educational community or teaching setting. Over more than thirty-five years of teaching, there have been current and former students whose friendship have enriched my life and that of my family where educational sharing extends into social interactions that are appropriate and mutually edifying. Care of students can deepen into professional and social contacts so that former students become colleagues and friends throughout one's lifetime. This has been a blessing that celebrates the need for social networks in the human community. For me the progression of student and mentee has developed to colleague and friend as a relationship deepens with a select number of current and former students. Such relationships honor the place of mutual ministry and edification in the Christian church. The friendship of *philia* relates to

---

[80] Amy Pollack, *The Course of Nature: A Book of Drawings on Natural Selection and Its Consequences*, with Commentary by Robert Pollack, (New York: Stonycreek Press, 2014), 111.

[81] See William and Aida Spencer, et. al., *Marriage at the Crossroads: Couples in Conversation About Discipleship, Gender Roles, Decision Making and Intimacy* (Downers Grove, Ill.: IVP Academic, 2009). Robert and Wanda Pazmiño wrote a chapter "Marriage for a North American Hispanic Couple," pp. 189-192, in this work.

bonds that persons have with their extended families where friends become close as family members.

The love of *caritas* is the kindness and hospitality extended to strangers about whom Jesus taught in the Parable of the Good Samaritan (Luke 10:25-37). In their initial encounters, students and teachers may well be strangers to each other. Maxine Greene suggests that teachers themselves can serve as provocative strangers who foster a sense of wonder with their students.[82] In this way teachers are both welcoming and supportive of students encountered as strangers, and provocative in posing challenges, problems and issues never imagined along with space for wonder and awe. In following Jesus' example, teachers can express and model concerns for the strangers and *anawim* in contemporary life as he noted in the case of the Good Samaritan.

The nature of *agape* in the teaching relationship focuses on the self-giving and sacrificial love that can undergird a teaching ministry with the distinction between *philia* and *agape* converging. This love is motivated by the Holy Spirit and is exemplified in life and ministry of Jesus during his earthly journey. Jesus' words to his disciples in John 15:12-16 capture a transition in his relationship with them:

> This is my commandment, that you love one another as I have loved you. No one has greater love than this, to lay down one's life for one's friends. You are my friends if you do what I command you. I do not call you servants any longer, because the servant does not know what the master is doing; but I have called you friends, because I have made known to you everything that I have heard from my Father. You did not choose me but I chose you. And I appointed you to go and bear fruit, fruit that will last, so that the Father will give you whatever you ask him in my name.

Jesus' fulfillment of God's plan to incarnate love in human flesh incorporates his followers as friends rather than servants. They are called to love as Jesus himself loved. A new commandment is to guide their relationships and for teachers the "one another" in this text includes their students. The Holy Spirit enables the proper expression of this love avoiding the dangers of *eros*, and fulfilling the expression of *agape* and in some cases, the experience of *philia* on the part of teachers in relationship with their students.

The classic text that describes the nature of *agape* for Christian understanding is First Corinthians chapter thirteen as eloquently

---

[82] Maxine Greene, *Teacher as Stranger: Educational Philosophy for the Modern Age* (Belmont, CA: Wadsworth, 1973).

composed by the Apostle Paul who exemplified caring relationships with his disciples:

> If I speak in the tongues of mortals and of angels, but do not have love, I am a noisy gong or a clanging cymbal. And if I have prophetic powers, and understand all mysteries and all knowledge, and if I have all faith, so as to remove mountains, but do not have love, I am nothing. If I give away all my possessions, and if I hand over my body so that I may boast, but do not have love, I gain nothing.
>
> Love is patient; love is kind; love is not envious or boastful or arrogant or rude. It does not insist on its own way; it is not irritable or resentful; it does not rejoice in wrongdoing, but rejoices in the truth. It bears all things, believes all things, hopes all things, endures all things.
>
> Love never ends. But as for prophecies, they will come to an end; as for tongues, they will cease; as for knowledge, it will come to an end. For we know only in part, and we prophesy only in part; but when the complete comes, the partial will come to an end. When I was a child, I spoke like a child, I thought like a child, I reasoned like a child; when I became an adult, I put an end to childish ways. For now we see in a mirror, dimly, but then we will see face to face. Now I know only in part; then I will know fully, even as I have been fully known. And now faith, hope, and love abide, these three; and the greatest of these is love.

Here is an insightful account regarding how *agape* love functions in relationships that can certainly include how teachers interact with their students. Love in teaching is demonstrated in the care taken to understand our students, the care taken to prepare the content and the context where teaching is undertaken. Love in teaching is demonstrated in the preparation of our heart, soul, mind and strength for the teaching occasion allowing adequate time for prayer to undergird the effort and asking for the Spirit's partnership.[83] No easy shortcuts are proposed for this level of care that wrestles with a host of other demands upon the time and commitments of teachers. With reliance upon God's Spirit comes the recognition that God can work despite our real limitations and weaknesses in terms of both preparation and actual instruction with the learning possible in evaluation.

## Paul and Jesus on Love

Teachers would do well to consider Paul's admonition in Galatians 5:13-15:

---

[83] See Robert W. Pazmiño, *Basics of Teaching for Christians: Preparation, Instruction and Evaluation* (Grand Rapids: Baker Books, 1998), 15-46, for a discussion of care or love in the preparation for teaching.

For you were called to freedom, brothers and sisters; only do not use your freedom as an opportunity for self-indulgence, but through love become slaves to one another. For the whole law is summed up in a single commandment, "You shall love your neighbor as yourself." If, however, you bite and devour one another, take care that you are not consumed by one another.

The freedom for love in Christian teaching according to Paul harkens back to Jesus' two great commandments with the second taking precedence for how teachers relate to students. Teachers need to see their students as their neighbors and even in the case of some students who may be existentially viewed as enemies, Jesus' commandment to love our enemies applies from the first teaching block or unit recorded in the Sermon on the Mount with Matthew as a helpful catechetical gospel:

"You have heard that it was said, 'You shall love your neighbor and hate your enemy.' But I say to you, Love your enemies and pray for those who persecute you, so that you may be children of your Father in heaven; for he makes his sun rise on the evil and on the good, and sends rain on the righteous and on the unrighteous. For if you love those who love you, what reward do you have? Do not even the tax collectors do the same? And if you greet only your brothers and sisters, what more are you doing than others? Do not even the Gentiles do the same? Be perfect, therefore, as your heavenly Father is perfect. (Matt 5:43-48)

It helps to note that the sense of perfection present in Jesus' teaching here in Matthew. Perfection (derived from Greek *teleios* referring to an end or goal) is the basic attitude of a believer, one of self-disinterested love (*agape*) and kindness for others, even for those who deserve no kindness, rather than absolute sinlessness on the part of teachers. We draw from God, from Jesus and the Spirit the grace to maintain this kind of love in our educational relationships.[84] Every teacher confronts a student who challenges us to rely upon spiritual resources to freely love them in our ministries. Teaching is a means for conveying God's love and care in concrete ways in the lives of students.

---

[84] Harold Lindsell, *Harper Study Bible* (Grand Rapids: Zondervan, 1971), 1445.

## Theological Reflections

Clark Pinnock in his work *Flame of Love*[85] helps to reframe pneumatology in ways that integrate the biblical perspectives of both Jesus and Paul. His understanding of the Holy Spirit honors the social doctrine of the Trinity, with God as pure relationality who seeks to draw all things into the symphony of love that is played eternally within the divine life. The triune God whose very being is an eternal dance of love, celebrates the Spirit's attempts to bring the entire creation by grace into that dance begun at creation and culminating at the consummation as discussed in chapter one of this work.[86] Pinnock invites a consideration of the Spirit's work in all of creation today because the Spirit sustains and invigorates all of life through the flame of love. The Spirit's love is manifest in miraculous processes of redemption and healing, but also in natural process of healing, including acts of social justice and reconciliation.[87] From Pinnock's understanding, it is essential to honor the freedom of the Spirit and God's use of means of grace in everyday life. Teaching itself then can be appreciated as a sacrament, a means of grace communicating God's love in Christ for the entire world (John 3:16).[88]

Teaching via Pinnock can be viewed as a dance in partnership with the Spirit that communicates God's love in Christ, even in confronting sin and suffering with the radical transformation and reconciliation possible in the Gospel.[89] It is God who sends the Spirit in the name of Jesus to teach us (John 14:26).[90] The Paraclete is a personal agent, teacher and friend to both teachers and students alike.[91] The Spirit is the tutor who accompanies each person in the educational exchange. All creatures are dependent on God for their life and strength, and it is God's Spirit who introduces love into the world, who sustains life and gives meaning.[92] The anointing by the Spirit is central for understanding the person and work of Jesus and if Jesus relied upon the Spirit's anointing, so should those who follow him and teach in Jesus' name.[93] The Christian church is an extension, not so much of the incarnation, as of the

---

[85] Clark H. Pinnock, *Flame of Love: A Theology of the Holy Spirit* (Downers Grove, Ill.: InterVarsity Press, 1996).
[86] Frank D. Macchia, "Tradition and the *Novum* of the Spirit: A Review of Clark Pinnock's *Flame of Love.*" *Journal of Pentecostal Theology* 13(1998), 34.
[87] Ibid, 38.
[88] Ibid, 46.
[89] Ibid, 38.
[90] Pinnock, *Flame of Love*, 28.
[91] Ibid, 35.
[92] Ibid, 51.
[93] Ibid, 79.

anointing of Jesus who serves as the church's exemplar or prototype.[94] At Pentecost the church received the Spirit and became the historical continuation of Jesus' anointing as the Christ.[95] The Spirit clothes persons with power to liberate people from oppression, to restore the community, to transform life and to instill hope as is beautifully described in the national renewal noted in Nehemiah 8 and discussed in chapter eleven of this work. The Spirit removes veils to disclose the truth (2 Cor 3:16-18) and offer alternatives that God graciously offers to all of humanity and creation.[96] Love involves willingness to confront the destroyers of life that stand in opposition to God's designs from the beginning of creation and made most clear in the new creation centered in Jesus Christ. What practical implications emerge from a pneumatology that celebrates God's love manifested cosmically in Jesus Christ?

**Practical Implications for Teaching**

Love is practiced by teachers initially by the level of commitment and dedication demonstrated well before entering any classroom or teaching relationship. The example of Ezra is noteworthy in this regard: "for Ezra had set his heart to study the law of the Lord, and to do it, and to teach the statutes and ordinances in Israel." (Ezra 7:10) Ezra's ministry is elaborated upon in chapter eleven. Careful attention to preparation for teaching demonstrates love where care is taken in relation to the content and experiences planned in relation to the persons of the students learning, their backgrounds and interests, and in relation to the context of teaching. Preparation includes regular times of prayer asking God's Spirit to work in the actual teaching and more importantly, in the hearts and lives of students. The preparation of persons must include the person of the teacher herself or himself. The heart, soul, mind and strength of the teachers must be spiritually quickened to support responsiveness and clarity in the act of teaching if it is to show students how to live, love and die in partnership with God.

Beyond preparation, love is demonstrated in instruction itself through clear communication, careful listening and civil dialogue. Listening to students honors the reality that the Spirit may be speaking more apparently and appropriately through other students than through the teacher's words. Love is demonstrated in the extent to which cooperative and collaborative learning transpires in a teaching event. Space must be allowed for what Parker Palmer describes as where "the community of

---

[94] Ibid, 114.
[95] Ibid, 118.
[96] Ibid, 163.

truth is practiced."[97] In teaching caring enough to affirm and confront students in relationship to the truth and its claims on our lives is a manifestation of love.

The evaluation of teaching is a third phase to allow for love to be freely practiced. Taking time and space to reflect upon learning and for students to gain perspective in the educational journey, demonstrates care for the transfer of classroom or occasional learning into everyday life where new truths can be tested and confirmed or discounted. This involves the taking of risks that cannot be avoided in any loving relationship where teaching fosters a freedom for love.

Love that immerses the preparation, instruction and evaluation of teaching requires a partnership with the Holy Spirit sustained through prayer, self-care and faith practices including regular times for worship and service beyond any classroom setting.

---

[97] Parker Palmer, *To Know As We Are Known: Education as a Spiritual Journey* (San Francisco: Harper San Francisco, 1993), xii.

CHAPTER 8

# Teaching and Freedom for Faith
Robert W. Pazmiño

Freedom for faith issues in service and mission within the Christian community and the wider world. Faith finds expression in lived actions as exemplified in the lives of heroes and heroines of the Christian faith described in the Book of Hebrews and chapter eleven of that New Testament book in particular. Faith also finds expression in a host of works that the Book of James suggests are essential to a living faith rather than one that is dead or lifeless (James 1:2-27; 2:14-26). But prior to an exploration of those key biblical frameworks for faith and its free expression and out working in the lives of faithful persons, the definition of faith itself looms as essential.

## What Is Faith?

The definition of faith has been discussed in relation to teaching and the attempt to designate stages of faith or styles of faith that vary across the life span. The ability to anticipate faith dynamics and issues intends to enhance the nurturing and formation of individual's faith and their relationships within particular faith communities that seek to pass along a living faith heritage across the generations. The historic work of both James Fowler in *Stages of Faith*[98] where he sought to delineate stages from the faith stories of persons, and of John Westerhoff in *Will Our Children Have Faith?*[99] where he sought to identify distinct styles of faith to guide formation efforts, stand out for consideration. In the case of Fowler, faith as a verb connected to life narratives was preferred to the traditional understanding of faith as a gift of God made available to humanity through grace and resulting in spiritual responses of individuals. In the case of Westerhoff, the progression of faith styles was helpfully compared with the growth rings of trees as they are nourished over time and only seen in the dissection of their trunks. Both efforts

---

[98] James W. Fowler, *Stages of Faith: The Psychology of Human Development and the Quest for Meaning* (San Francisco: Harper & Row, 1981), 117-213.
[99] John H. Westerhoff, *Will Our Children Have Faith?* (New York: Seabury, 1976), 89-91.

provided intellectual instrumentalities to guide the ministry of faithful teachers who seek to nurture faith in those exploring and embracing the Christian faith as disciples of Jesus. Jesus promised the coming of the Holy Spirit to guide his followers in their faith (John 14:15-31; 15:26-27; 16:4-15).

Faith in biblical usage within the Christian tradition is noteworthy as found in Hebrews 11:1 "Now faith is the assurance of things hoped for, the conviction of things not seen." Faith in this case suggests assurance and conviction on the part of human persons, but begs the question regarding the object and subject of that assurance and conviction. The passage of Hebrews 11 quoted in full here provides insights that the object of that faith of persons is the living God, and the subjects of that faith include the relationships between persons and God revealed to them:

> Now faith is the assurance of things hoped for, the conviction of things not seen. Indeed, by faith our ancestors received approval. By faith we understand that the worlds were prepared by the word of God, so that what is seen was made from things that are not visible. By faith Abel offered to God a more acceptable sacrifice than Cain's. Through this he received approval as righteous, God himself giving approval to his gifts; he died, but through his faith he still speaks. By faith Enoch was taken so that he did not experience death; and "he was not found, because God had taken him." For it was attested before he was taken away that "he had pleased God." And without faith it is impossible to please God, for whoever would approach him must believe that he exists and that he rewards those who seek him.
>
> By faith Noah, warned by God about events as yet unseen, respected the warning and built an ark to save his household; by this he condemned the world and became an heir to the righteousness that is in accordance with faith. By faith Abraham obeyed when he was called to set out for a place that he was to receive as an inheritance; and he set out, not knowing where he was going. By faith he stayed for a time in the land he had been promised, as in a foreign land, living in tents, as did Isaac and Jacob, who were heirs with him of the same promise. For he looked forward to the city that has foundations, whose architect and builder is God. By faith he received power of procreation, even though he was too old—and Sarah herself was barren—because he considered him faithful who had promised. Therefore from one person, and this one as good as dead, descendants were born, "as many as the stars of heaven and as the innumerable grains of sand by the seashore."
>
> All of these died in faith without having received the promises, but from a distance they saw and greeted them. They confessed that they were strangers and foreigners on the earth, for people who speak in this

way make it clear that they are seeking a homeland. If they had been thinking of the land that they had left behind, they would have had opportunity to return. But as it is, they desire a better country, that is, a heavenly one. Therefore God is not ashamed to be called their God; indeed, he has prepared a city for them.

By faith Abraham, when put to the test, offered up Isaac. He who had received the promises was ready to offer up his only son, of whom he had been told, "It is through Isaac that descendants shall be named for you." He considered the fact that God is able even to raise someone from the dead—and figuratively speaking, he did receive him back. By faith Isaac invoked blessings for the future on Jacob and Esau. By faith Jacob, when dying, blessed each of the sons of Joseph, "bowing in worship over the top of his staff." By faith Joseph, at the end of his life, made mention of the exodus of the Israelites and gave instructions about his burial. By faith Moses was hidden by his parents for three months after his birth, because they saw that the child was beautiful; and they were not afraid of the king's edict. By faith Moses, when he was grown up, refused to be called a son of Pharaoh's daughter, choosing rather to share ill-treatment with the people of God than to enjoy the fleeting pleasures of sin. He considered abuse suffered for the Christ to be greater wealth than the treasures of Egypt, for he was looking ahead to the reward. By faith he left Egypt, unafraid of the king's anger; for he persevered as though he saw him who is invisible. By faith he kept the Passover and the sprinkling of blood, so that the destroyer of the firstborn would not touch the firstborn of Israel. By faith the people passed through the Red Sea as if it were dry land, but when the Egyptians attempted to do so they were drowned. By faith the walls of Jericho fell after they had been encircled for seven days.

By faith Rahab the prostitute did not perish with those who were disobedient, because she had received the spies in peace.

And what more should I say? For time would fail me to tell of Gideon, Barak, Samson, Jephthah, of David and Samuel and the prophets— who through faith conquered kingdoms, administered justice, obtained promises, shut the mouths of lions, quenched raging fire, escaped the edge of the sword, won strength out of weakness, became mighty in war, put foreign armies to flight.

Women received their dead by resurrection. Others were tortured, refusing to accept release, in order to obtain a better resurrection. Others suffered mocking and flogging, and even chains and imprisonment. They were stoned to death, they were sawn in two, they were killed by the sword; they went about in skins of sheep and goats, destitute, persecuted, tormented—of whom the world was not worthy. They wandered in deserts and mountains, and in caves and holes in the ground. Yet all these, though they were commended for their faith, did not receive what was promised, since God had provided something better so that they would not, apart from us, be made perfect.

Within this rich exposition of faith by the writer of Hebrews, verse 2 makes explicit that the relationship between God and persons is essential for faith to be free and to find expression and that the approval of God is at stake. Verse 3 suggests that understanding is important and relates to loving God with all of one's mind in one's life journey. This love invites continual learning, recalling that the key meaning of a disciple is a learner. Faith then is evidenced in the lives of faithful persons whose witness here includes Abel, Enoch, Noah, Abraham, Isaac, Jacob, Joseph, Moses' parents, Moses and the people, a mixed crowd who are following him, Rahab, Gideon, Barak, Samson, Jephthah, David, Samuel, prophets and women (vv. 4-35). The text notes those who suffered greatly, those who wandered in deserts, mountains, caves and holes in their journeys, along with those not delivered from great trials and even death for their faith (vv. 35-40). All are commended and promised God's provision despite their diverse experiences. In this extensive recounting of exemplary faithful persons, some though limited mention of women can be noted with only Rehab named. The names of Sarah, Hagar, Rebekah, Rachel, Leah, Miriam, Shiphrah, Puah, Deborah, Huldah and Esther could well be added along with a host of others like Mary, Martha, and Mary Magdalene from New Testament accounts.

In addition to Hebrews' listing of faith figures, what is noted in Ephesians 2: 8-10 assists in understanding the significance of faith:

> For by grace you have been saved through faith, and this is not your own doing; it is the gift of God—not the result of works, so that no one may boast. For we are what he has made us, created in Christ Jesus for good works, which God prepared beforehand to be our way of life.

Faith is the human response to God's gracious gift of Jesus Christ. With Paul's authorship of Ephesians, faith is clearly identified as a gift of God to persons and not the result of their works, and yet the free expression of that gift of faith results in good works that followers of Jesus perform in their lives. Here is a confirmation of the essential teaching of the Book of James that makes explicit the connection of faith with the actions or works of Christians in their service, mission and outreach in the world. It is into the world with all of its challenges, trails and tests, that Christians are sent to live out their faith. (James 1:2-27; 2:14-26). James 1 notes:

> My brothers and sisters, whenever you face trials of any kind, consider
> it nothing but joy,
> because you know that the testing of your faith produces endurance;

and let endurance have its full effect, so that you may be mature and complete, lacking in nothing.

If any of you is lacking in wisdom, ask God, who gives to all generously and ungrudgingly, and it will be given you.

But ask in faith, never doubting, for the one who doubts is like a wave of the sea, driven and tossed by the wind;

for the doubter, being double-minded and unstable in every way, must not expect to receive anything from the Lord.

Let the believer who is lowly boast in being raised up,

and the rich in being brought low, because the rich will disappear like a flower in the field.

For the sun rises with its scorching heat and withers the field; its flower falls, and its beauty perishes. It is the same way with the rich; in the midst of a busy life, they will wither away.

Blessed is anyone who endures temptation. Such a one has stood the test and will receive the crown of life that the Lord has promised to those who love him.

No one, when tempted, should say, "I am being tempted by God"; for God cannot be tempted by evil and he himself tempts no one.

But one is tempted by one's own desire, being lured and enticed by it;

then, when that desire has conceived, it gives birth to sin, and that sin, when it is fully grown, gives birth to death.

Do not be deceived, my beloved.

Every generous act of giving, with every perfect gift, is from above, coming down from the Father of lights, with whom there is no variation or shadow due to change.

In fulfillment of his own purpose he gave us birth by the word of truth, so that we would become a kind of first fruits of his creatures.

You must understand this, my beloved: let everyone be quick to listen, slow to speak, slow to anger;

for your anger does not produce God's righteousness.

Therefore, rid yourselves of all sordidness and rank growth of wickedness, and welcome with meekness the implanted word that has the power to save your souls.

But be doers of the word, and not merely hearers who deceive themselves.

For if any are hearers of the word and not doers, they are like those who look at themselves in a mirror;

for they look at themselves and, on going away, immediately forget what they were like.

But those who look into the perfect law, the law of liberty, and persevere, being not hearers who forget but doers who act—they will be blessed in their doing.

If any think they are religious, and do not bridle their tongues but deceive their hearts, their religion is worthless.

Religion that is pure and undefiled before God, the Father, is this: to care for orphans and widows in their distress, and to keep oneself unstained by the world (v.2-27).

This passage connects faith and action; hearers of faithful words are called to be doers of faithful acts in the world. The testing of faith, so well exemplified in lives of those noted in the Hebrews account, were doers. They, like us, are admonished to ask for wisdom in faith to guide our decisions and actions. The care for orphans and widows, and purity in one's life following self-examination with discerning speech are evidences of faith. Also being quick to listen and slow to speak and anger, are all faithful actions clearly noted in this passage. James' instructions for faithful living continue in chapter 2:

What good is it, my brothers and sisters, if you say you have faith but do not have works? Can faith save you?
If a brother or sister is naked and lacks daily food,
and one of you says to them, "Go in peace; keep warm and eat your fill," and yet you do not supply their bodily needs, what is the good of that?
So faith by itself, if it has no works, is dead.
But someone will say, "You have faith and I have works." Show me your faith apart from your works, and I by my works will show you my faith.
You believe that God is one; you do well. Even the demons believe— and shudder.
Do you want to be shown, you senseless person, that faith apart from works is barren?
Was not our ancestor Abraham justified by works when he offered his son Isaac on the altar?
You see that faith was active along with his works, and faith was brought to completion by the works.
Thus the scripture was fulfilled that says, "Abraham believed God, and it was reckoned to him as righteousness," and he was called the friend of God.
You see that a person is justified by works and not by faith alone.
Likewise, was not Rahab the prostitute also justified by works when she welcomed the messengers and sent them out by another road?
For just as the body without the spirit is dead, so faith without works is also dead (v.14-26).

A living faith finds expression in the lives of believers. From the Hebrews hall of fame for the faithful exemplars, Abraham and Rahab are singled out for our consideration. Their lives give witness to an integrity between their confessions of faith and their actions in life. Their faith issues in works of service accomplishing at great personal risk God's mission in the world. The Holy Spirit is the partner in these ventures or works that issue from faith in diverse settings where persons follow the promptings or guidance of the Spirit. The Holy Spirit actively cooperates with human spirits attuned to God's continuous activities in time and space to accomplish God's will and purposes outlined in God's Word. This partnership with the Holy Spirit is modeled in the life, death and resurrection of Jesus Christ.[100] What enabled persons to experience freedom for their faith?

## Freedom for Faith?

The freedom for faith celebrated in Hebrews 11 raises the question of whether freedom itself exists in the exercise of faith. The writer assumes a freedom of religion that paradoxically some may choose as a freedom from religion. As a person of faith, my concern is for religious freedom that allows for the full expression of faith and in my Baptist tradition soul liberty. Soul liberty allows for the following of conscience and the personal choice of religious belief, expression and practice across the wider community and society. The imposition and coercion of faith upon others is opposed while honoring the opportunity to share religious beliefs and practices. This sharing is to be protected provided it does not threaten the common good and universal human rights of others. Those rights are implicit in a biblical view of the worth and dignity of every human being who are created in God's image and therefore worthy of care and equal protection under the law. Freedom for faith assumes that faith itself is a gift made possible through the gracious working of the Holy Spirit upon human hearts, spirits and minds suggested by the theological dimensions of faith.

## Theological Dimensions of Faith

The reality of faith in teaching can be seen in relation to a traditional theological understanding of faith itself. Faith can be viewed in terms of the dimensions of *notitia* (intellectual affirmation), *assensus* (affective affirmation), and *fiducia* (intentional affirmation) and all these dimensions interact to foster a full embrace of God and the freedom God intends for humanity. The balance of freedom and form maintains a

---

[100] For one discussion of Jesus' model and teaching agenda, see Robert W. Pazmiño, *So What Makes Our Teaching Christian: Teaching in the Name, Spirit and Power of Jesus* (Eugene, OR: Wipf & Stock, 2008).

balance that affirms both ardor and order in faithful living. The intellectual, affective and intentional affirmations of faith rest upon the reality and revelation of God.

In relation to the intellectual dimension of faith, *notitia,* teachers are called to bring every thought captive to the mind of Christ as suggested by Second Corinthians 10:4b-5: "We destroy arguments and every proud obstacle raised up against the knowledge of God, and we take every thought captive to obey Christ." Having the mind of Christ calls for imitating his humility as the Philippians 2:5-8 passage teaches:

> Let the same mind be in you that was in Christ Jesus, who, though he was in the form of God, did not regard equality with God as something to be exploited, but emptied himself, taking the form of a slave, being born in human likeness. And being found in human form, he humbled himself and became obedient to the point of death—even death on a cross.

There is no place for intellectual pride in teaching, but seeking to love God with all of one's mind reflecting the glories of God's creation and divine and true wisdom that stands in stark contrast with human wisdom (Jas 3:13-18) as explored insightfully and in depth by Octavio Esqueda:

> The book of James provides us with the complete perspective about true wisdom and how it can become clear and evident to everybody around us. The well-known chapter 3 deals with the importance of the tongue and its great influence for good and evil. In fact, this passage stars with a severe warning for anyone who desires to become a teacher since teachers use their tongues as key instruments to provide instruction and, therefore, they become more susceptible of receiving a stricter judgment because of their possible misuse of their tongues.
>
> At the end of his vivid description about the tongue influence, James asks a very interesting question in verse 13, "Who among you is wise and understanding?" Posing this clear and direct interrogation, James confronts us with the complete meaning of wisdom. The answer he provides is surprising for our common standards because he argues that wisdom goes far beyond knowledge or understanding "Let him show by his good behavior his deeds in the gentleness of wisdom." True wisdom, James reminds us, becomes evident in our behavior. Unfortunately, in the higher education world is uncommon to find highly educated scholars who are also humble at the same time. When this combination happens, these people become the exceptions when in reality they should be norm, especially in Christian higher education.

James also contrasts the wisdom that reflects the Creator and the one that goes completely against the divine ideal. James is very direct and clearly describes the characteristics of ungodly wisdom, "But if you have bitter jealousy and selfish ambition in your heart, do not be arrogant and *so* lie against the truth. This wisdom is not that which comes down from above, but is earthly, natural, demonic. For where jealousy and selfish ambition exist, there is disorder and every evil thing" (James 3:14-16).

On the other hand, godly wisdom manifests the following characteristics, "But the wisdom from above is first pure, then peaceable, gentle, reasonable, full of mercy and good fruits, unwavering, without hypocrisy. And the seed whose fruit is righteousness is sown in peace by those who make peace" (James 3:17-18).

Therefore, wise people demonstrate their wisdom through their behavior not through their knowledge or academic achievements. According to James, jealously and selfish ambition describe an earthly, natural, and demonic wisdom that completely misrepresents the Lord of the universe. These severe words are a strong warning against denominational, ecclesial, and academic disputes. True wisdom encourages peace and cordiality. Wise people are peaceful and those around them find refreshment in their presence.

Authentic wisdom is within everybody reach and at the same time is always hard to attain. As the Scriptures reminds us, knowledge can produce arrogance, but love always edifies. It is my deep desire that my students, and everybody around me, could sincerely say about me "magister meus doctus est" when they observe my behavior. How wise are you? You do not need to answer this question using words, you are already doing it with your life and it is evident to everybody. [101]

Freedom for faith includes the freedom of thought and can be related to academic freedom in school settings on the part of teachers and freedom for critical and creative thought and reflection on the part of students. These commitments involve allowing for questions and genuine searching for the truth in educational practices that ought to include sufficient opportunity for dialogue that is extended with increased maturity and experience of participants.

The freedom for faith in relation to *assensus* can celebrate freedom while also honoring the form of the Christian faith which for me is embodied in one historic formulation such as the Apostles' Creed:

---

[101] See Octavio J. Esqueda's helpful discussion of this text at the Talbot School of Theology Good Book Blog: https://www.biola.edu/blogs/good-book-blog/2011/my-professor-is-wise

I believe in God, the Father almighty,
creator of heaven and earth.
I believe in Jesus Christ, his only Son, our Lord,
who was conceived by the Holy Spirit
and born of the virgin Mary.
He suffered under Pontius Pilate,
was crucified, died, and was buried;
he descended to hell.
The third day he rose again from the dead.
He ascended to heaven
and is seated at the right hand of God the Father almighty.
From there he will come to judge the living and the dead.
I believe in the Holy Spirit,
the holy catholic church,
the communion of saints,
the forgiveness of sins,
the resurrection of the body,
and the life everlasting. Amen.

Though being from a non-creedal Protestant tradition, I find that the creed helps to delineate key beliefs to guide teaching.[102] Intellectual affirmation of the faith expands upon this foundation to consider varieties of persons, communities, traditions and contexts.

The affective dimension of faith, *assensus*, finds expression in teaching through the heart-felt affirmation of God's revelation of care and lament in relation to God's creation and humanity's plight. Because God cares for persons and the restoration of fellowship made possible in Jesus Christ through the ministry of the Holy Spirit, teachers extend that care in their relationships with students and the wider community and society. The expression of lamentation is appropriate in the light of human suffering that includes all of creation that groans until God's promised consummation is experienced:

We know that the whole creation has been groaning in labor pains until now; and not only the creation, but we ourselves, who have been the first fruits of the Spirit, groan inwardly while we wait for adoption, the redemption of our bodies. (Rom 8:22-23)

---

[102] See my discussion using the Apostles' Creed in Robert W. Pazmiño, *Foundational Issues in Christian Education: An Introduction in Evangelical Perspective.* 3rd ed. (Grand Rapids: Baker Academic, 2008), pp. 69-72.

The expression of our feelings relates to loving God with all of our heart and soul that is attended to in the affective dimension of teaching (Luke 10:27).[103] Freedom of emotional expression nurtures creativity, imagination, and artistic expression modeled in the ministries of both Bezalel and Oholiab in the Hebrew Scriptures (Exo 31:2-5; 35:30-34; 38:23). Both the artistic works of Bezalel and Oholiab are described as being anointed by God's Spirit and their teaching of their crafts to others in the adornment of the tabernacle, the place of communal worship.

The intentional dimension of faith, *fiducia*, relates to the matter of commitment, devotion and discipline. One exemplary model for this faithful devotion is found in Ezra, the scribe whom God used to provide leadership during a time of struggle and transition in the life of Israel. As noted in Ezra 7:10: "Ezra had set his heart to study the law of the Lord, and to do it, and to teach that statutes and ordinances in Israel." The setting of the heart speaks of devotion, dedication, and commitment even at personal cost to Ezra. The matter of devotion and commitment is a major challenge in an age that glorifies personal comfort and pleasure. Faithful service can be demanding and costly and too often avoided with a preference for the quick fix in all areas of personal and public life. The model of Jesus' life especially in terms of the cross poses a distinct alternative to many cultural norms and preferred practices in both personal and corporate life (Luke 9:23).

A noteworthy exception to this cultural pattern of narcissism is what women in many local and global settings have been expected to fulfill in their caring for others. Carol Lakey Hess exposes this pattern in *Caretakers of Our Common House* where self-sacrifice becomes a sin at the expense of the self-development of women.[104] Christian teachers of both genders need to be caretakers of our own house (self) as well as our common house (faith community and world). In this effort our intentions and commitments need to be as clear as possible. In addition the love of neighbor requires a component of self-love or self-care so as not to be depleted and care-weary in areas of service and mission. *Fiducia* and freedom for its exercise implies a freedom of choice within limits. Choices are to be edifying and contributing to the life of community for no person is an island unto themselves as is evident in all of creation and its web of interdependence. Faith has an intergenerational character if it is to be sustained over time in faith communities. The personal areas of

---

[103] See Mary Elizabeth Mullino Moore, *Teaching from the Heart: Theology and Educational Method* (Harrisburg, Pa.: Trinity Press International, 1998) who addresses the quality of teaching in referring to the heart in receiving and giving the Spirit of Life (p. ix).
[104] Carol Lakey Hess, *Caretakers of our Common House: Women's Development in Communities of Faith* (Nashville: Abingdon, 1997), 38.

choice include communal, corporate and systemic dimensions of life that will be explored in part three of this volume. Freedom for faith honors the liberty God intended for persons to explore and mature across their life spans accompanied by God's Spirit in their journeys.

Faith basically involves trust in God. An acrostic from my Sunday school years growing up in Brooklyn, New York outlined the following:

**F**orsaking
**A**ll
**I**
**T**rust
**H**im

The acrostic was well rooted in one of my favorite memory verses from Proverbs 3:5-6: "Trust in the LORD with all thine heart; and lean not unto thine own understanding. In all thy ways acknowledge him, and he shall direct thy paths." (KJV) Trusting in God was to bear fruits and find expression in all ways of living and shared both personally and communally.

CHAPTER 9

# Teaching and Freedom for Hope
Robert W. Pazmiño

Christian teaching involves a number of risks and factors that call for careful consideration and celebration. Teaching that discloses and discovers truth can readily lead to a sense of hopelessness in relation to current realities and challenges. In contrast, the Christian faith has historically affirmed along with the Apostle Paul "Now the Lord is the Spirit, and where the Spirit of the Lord is, there is freedom" (2 Cor 3:17). This freedom finds expression in hope among other Christian virtues. Jesus in his first public teaching recorded in Luke 4:18-19 proclaims a message of hope to his immediate hearers:

> The Spirit of the Lord is upon me, because he has anointed me to bring good news to the poor. He has sent me to proclaim release to the captives and recovery of sight to the blind, to let the oppressed go free, to proclaim the year of the Lord's favor.

By exploring the resources of God and the transformative ministry of the Holy Spirit, teachers who follow Jesus can provide alternatives to a sense of hopelessness and despair many encounter in their life journeys, especially those who are marginalized and underserved by the wider society. Christian educators are called to rest in God who graciously works despite, through and beyond us in our partnership with God's Spirit who is active in the world and inviting hopeful ventures to sustain life as God intends it.[105] The biblical accounts of our Christian hope serve to guide and ground the effort to embrace the freedom for hope in teaching.

## Biblical Accounts

For Christians, our adoption into God's family with its present and future blessings is sealed through the sign and seal of God's Spirit that is

---

[105] See Robert W. Pazmiño, *God Our Teacher: Theological basics in Christian Education* (Grand Rapids: Baker Academic, 2001) for a discussion of God being despite, through and beyond us.

the first fruit of our Christian inheritance. Paul describes this legacy in Romans 8:15-17:

> For you did not receive a spirit that makes you a slave again to fear, but you received the Spirit of sonship (or adoption) and by him we cry, "*Abba* Father." The Spirit himself testifies with our spirit that we are God's children. Now if we are children, then we are heirs—heirs of God and co-heirs with Christ, if indeed we share in his sufferings in order that we may also share in his glory.

Paul also in his letter to the Ephesians makes this connection with our spiritual inheritance shared by followers of Jesus:

> And you also were included in Christ when you heard the word of truth, the gospel of your salvation. Having believed, you were marked in him with a seal, the promised Holy Spirit, who is a deposit guaranteeing our inheritance until the redemption of those who are God's possession—to the praise of his glory (Eph 1:13-14).

Adoption and the gift of the Holy Spirit confront the culture of fear with an inheritance of hope, assurance and courage to address all of life's challenges with others in community. Christian educators in their ministry hope that through the time shared with others in learning, lives can be transformed by the Spirit in ways that glorify God and renew all the creation. Such transformation is a source of joy and offers hope to all generations across the life span. The Apostle Paul makes explicit the ministry of hope in relation to the Holy Spirit: "and hope does disappoint us, because God's love has been poured into our hearts through the Holy Spirit that has been given to us" (Romans 5:5). Our blessed hope in Christ who one day will destroy pain, suffering, and death forever is an important one to keep in mind as we live and teach with hope today (Rev 21:1-7). One example of teaching and freedom for hope comes from a ministry experience in East Harlem, New York.

## Ministry Example

From my ministry experience in East Harlem, New York, from 1972 to 1981, I personally witnessed the fruits of faithful mentoring and congregational educational support that nurtured the future ministries of Rev. Luis Cortes and his brother Rev. Danny Cortes who now lead *Esperanza* (Hope) ministries in Philadelphia, Pennsylvania. They are having a significant national impact in the United States and also a global impact in Panama with Schools of Hope established in that Central

American country. The implicit messages given to Hispanic youth in New York during the seventies were that they were members of what popular media later identified as the "permanent underclass" of U. S. society. The congregational teaching the youth received freed them from limited expectations for inner-city Hispanic youth to pursue ministries bringing hope to a host of other youth, their families and entire communities nationally and now internationally.

Luis and Danny were former members of the youth/young adult group at the Second Spanish Baptist Church located in East Harlem, New York where I served as a youth/young adult counselor along with a dedicated couple, Jaime and Iris Rivera, who had three of their own children active in the group. Direct youth ministry was conducted during the years of 1972 through 1981 with what later emerged as a team of lay leaders trained in our home. Former theological students from my graduate teaching at Andover Newton Theological School have also provided leadership at Esperanza in networking with local churches and providing strong academic administration of a newly launched college (Esperanza College) for Hispanic students in the person of former Dean Elizabeth Conde-Frazier. These students were long excluded from contextualized college education, but now Esperanza College is affiliated with Eastern University and provides instruction in the students' first language of Spanish as well as English. In addition, other educational programs were launched including Esperanza Academy for high school students. *Esperanza* (Hope) is a model for equipping Hispanic communities, churches, families and persons in education and diverse public ministries. Luis himself offered the prayer at the luncheon following the second inauguration of President Barack Obama in January 2013 that publicly recognized the role that Hispanic voters and support played in his re-election.

From the sense of a limited and hopeless future, teaching equipped by the Holy Spirit enabled Hispanic youth to experience a freedom for hope and to engage their own spiritual imaginations to serve a community "suffering from poverty, unstable housing, low educational attainment and high crime." The efforts of Esperanza have included community and economic development, immigration, education as noted, capacity building, workforce development, health initiatives, and even climate initiatives in a comprehensive offering of hope for improving the lives of Hispanic families and other ethnic groups as well in the city of Philadelphia, known as the city of brotherly love.

One great teacher of the Christian faith tradition from North Africa, Augustine of Hippo, provided historical insights on the effort to secure the freedom for hope in Spirit-inspired and Spirit-anointed teaching.

## Augustine on Hope

Augustine observed that "Hope has two lovely daughters, anger and courage. Anger at the way things are, and courage to see that they need not remain as they are."[106] Anger can result from disclosing and discovering the truth as explored in chapter six of this work, anger at the way things are in contrast with God's intentions and purposes for humanity and all of creation. Besides Jesus and Paul in the Christian faith tradition, it is Augustine who stands as a highly influential teacher over the centuries for all Christians who teach.[107] The quote from Augustine has impacted my thoughts on Christian teaching because I too have two lovely daughters, one by birth and one by marriage. Rebekah is my daughter by birth. She is an attorney who advocates for the needs of those marginalized and seeking justice in the criminal system of New York City and State. She is in her thirties, majored during college in sociology and Latino studies, and has worked in the area of public defense advocacy at the appellate level in New York City and is currently working at Ryker's Island prison.

Larisa is my daughter by marriage. She was a development officer and grants writer for "Facing History and Ourselves" that is an international educational and professional organization whose mission is to engage students of diverse backgrounds in an examination of racism, prejudice, and anti-Semitism in order to promote the development of a more humane and informed society. She has also worked in the medical and higher educational fields in securing resources and medical care for all in need. Larisa is also the mother of my two grandchildren.

When I think of my daughters' lives and their vocational commitments, I think of hope for the future where the common good and need of others leads to lives of service in the wider public community. These ministries of hope are as significant as those centered in the local church and faith-based efforts such as Esperanza. The ministry of the laity along with the clergy is crucial to restore hope to the lives of persons all created in God's image and worthy of care.

How is it possible for Christian teaching to foster hope for children, youth and adults in their life circumstances, choices and vocations? The expression of anger and rage in the life of local and wider global communities is often related to a sense of hopelessness that many young people and adults may be experiencing in their lives and in a world

---

[106] As cited in Wilbert J. McKeachie, *Teaching Tips: Strategies, Research, and Theory for College and University Teachers*, 9th ed. (Lexington, Mass.: Heath, 1994), 384.

[107] Augustine while being influential can be critiqued for his separating the body and soul in his teaching and his distorted view of women and Jews evident in some of his writings.

preoccupied with numerous fears. Fears, for example, fuel the current culture of gun violence in the United States that has taken a high toll upon children and youth. This reality was brought before national consciousness in the tragedy of Newtown, Connecticut at Sandy Hook Elementary School on December 14, 2012 where twenty first-grade children and six school staff died. Adding to this tragedy was the death of Adam Lanza, the shooter himself and his mother. The choice before the United States as a nation is between life and death, between hope and destruction as historically outlined in Deuteronomy 30:11-20. The call issued from this passage for Israel, and by extension for all nations, is to confront the destroyers of life in one's culture. In the United States the choice is between the proliferation of gun violence and profits from the lucrative sale of weapons nationally and internationally, or the very lives of our children, youth and adults and their opportunity to thrive in relative safety in public places like schools, playgrounds, cinemas, churches, streets and sidewalks where they can play and learn. The First Amendment of the United States Constitution names the right of assembly requiring public safety and responsible gun control. On a recent trip with students to the Arizona/Mexico border for a course on immigration I learned that as human and drug trafficking move north across that border, gun trafficking moves south. Those guns support the very violence that is the primary motivation for bringing persons north that now includes children and families in increasing numbers.

Christian teaching offers freedom from fear and an alternative sense of hope for persons, families, groups and communities whether in East Harlem, New York, Newtown, Connecticut, Nogales, Arizona or Nogales, Mexico. The Apostle Paul in his letter to the Ephesians described the experiences of persons before coming to faith as "having no hope and without God in the world" (Eph 2:12). In his influential work *Race Matters*, Cornel West advocated for a politics of conversion that provides "a chance for people to believe there is hope for the future and a meaning to struggle" that religious faith itself provides.[108] West's politics apply to African Americans, and more broadly, to all folk who hunger for freedom, liberation and a new life. Those on the margins of society, those I identify as the *anawim* from the Scriptures, particularly hunger for an alternative life.[109] The anawim are those who are poor, humble, and/or weak before God and others, identified as the oppressed and marginalized in any setting. It was the *anawim* to whom Jesus as teacher paid particular attention in his earthly ministry.

---

[108] Cornel West, *Race Matters* (Boston: Beacon, 1993), 18.
[109] See my discussion of the *anawim* in Robert W. Pazmiño, *By What Authority Do we Teach? Sources for Empowering Christian Educators* (Grand Rapids: Baker, 1994), 63-65, 69, 77, 99, 144.

As faith educators we can ask ourselves: Who are those who feel life is hopeless? How can believers make a difference with those persons over time and embrace the need for advocacy in serving them and God in experiencing the abundant life about which Jesus so eloquently spoke (John 10:10)? How can our teaching raise awareness and serve to motivate students who are willing to work in partnership with the Holy Spirit in offering hope where it may not currently exist in a broken yet beloved world?

## Advocacy and Time Perspectives with Hope

Affirming the place of advocacy (speaking up for the *anawim*, for those marginalized) in teaching is an inherently hopeful venture. The Brazilian educator Paulo Freire pointed out the need for education in hope while embracing the teaching task of advocacy: "One of the tasks of the progressive educator is to unveil opportunities for hope, no matter what the obstacles be. We need critical hope the way a fish needs unpolluted water."[110] Advocacy involves confronting and countering the destroyers of life and giving voice to those who have been silenced over time and in their current settings. Included in those voices are those who lost their lives in Newtown and a host of others who have died as the result of gun violence daily in the United States and various forms of structural violence that destroy the possibilities for an abundant life as Jesus intended (John 10:10) for all persons.

In 1978 when I graduated from seminary, my first ministerial call came from my pastor, Reverend Santiago, to drive and accompany him and Raul Sanchez to the city morgue in New York City. We had to identify Elsa Sanchez, Raul's daughter, who had been murdered in the Polo Grounds Projects where Luis and Danny Cortes also lived. Elsa had just completed her first year in college and was the first member of her family to attend college. She was a youth I had taught and interacted with in both Sunday school and youth group for four years. She was a beautiful and outgoing young women who was about to start a summer position in community service. Urban ministries have long wrestled with violence that is increasingly evident in the suburbs, small idyllic towns and rural communities of the United States like Newtown, Connecticut.

A stance of advocacy is taken in the light of God's purposes for humankind and all of creation finding expression in the world. The vision of *shalom* that God discloses in the Scriptures embodies peace and a fullness of life for all of God's creation. Advocacy ministries call for

---

[110] Paulo Freire, *Pedagogy of Hope: Reliving Pedagogy of the Oppressed*, trans. Robert R. Barr (New York: Continuum, 1994), 9.

attention to the perception of time in human affairs in embracing a longed-for hope. Hope is typically associated with the future, but must also be seen in light of the past and present of our personal and communal lives.

A discussion of hope in relation to teaching raises the issue of our own time perspectives and how time configures into our thinking, acting and living. The faith educator Augustine wrote in his Confessions of "the present of things past, the present of things present, and the present of things in the future" in relation to life and ministry.[111] Whereas hope understandably focuses on the present of better things future, perspective is only provided in considering both the past and present in relation to that future through Christian teaching. Anticipation for the future is built upon memories of the past and current day attention to realities in the present time. The Spirit's ministry is present in the disclosure of the past with its shadows and lights, in the attention given to current challenging realities and in the anticipation of better times and possibilities calling for spiritual imagination.

Teaching can provide the needed reflective space and time to consider the future in connection with the all too forgotten past and pressing current needs. The past provides a source for identity and the reappropriation of living traditions with memories providing the manna for sustained living. In relation to the past, students can explore points of both continuity and change.

A two-week visit to China in 2000 with a delegation from Andover Newton Theological School convinced me again of a living hope as evidenced in the lives of Chinese Christians. They were sustained through the fiery trials of the Cultural Revolution as their churches and seminaries had reopened or were newly built to accommodate increasing numbers of youth and young adults with their spiritual hunger and calling. This hunger is being satisfied in the teaching and living of faith communities that both forms persons and allows a place for questions and doubts in relation to traditions revisited in the light of contemporary changes.

## A Place for Questions and Doubts in Extended Ventures of Hope

Teaching extends a formative ministry to enable followers of a religious tradition to mature in their faith and to express their faith commitments in the world. Initially this teaching includes the opportunity to explore and consider faith among a wide variety of

---

[111] Augustine of Hippo, *Augustine's Confessions* (Grand Rapids: Sovereign Grace, 1971), 114.

options in a pluralistic world. Teachers honor the place of questions and doubts as opportunities to wrestle with the full implications of any topic under discussion, encouraging both critical and creative thought guided by the Holy Spirit whom Jesus sent to lead us into all truth (John 15:26; 16:13). Dialogue in the Christian tradition enables persons to consider loving God, loving their neighbors and all of creation where hope extends into all of life with its ever-present challenges to inherited patterns and perspectives that need to be re-examined if life is to flourish.

Teaching can be an inherently hopeful ministry with the nurturing of spiritual imagination and courage to realize alternatives. It encourages participants to see, imagine and dream what God hopes for humanity and all of creation. It offers the possibility of new ventures of faith to those at different points in their life journeys. Accommodating and celebrating the gifts and questions of youth in East Harlem nurtured, in some imaginative ways, the ministries of hope in Philadelphia and across the United States. Participants' experiences and the level of their expertise vary in certain areas of faith study.

The youth at Second Baptist trained for, planned and implemented a summer day for children in the surrounding community as a result of a community walk one Sunday morning with children and youth to observe our setting and the needs of folk. Some of the church leaders strongly objected to such a community walk, even though it safely exposed children and youth to realities outside our very church doors. Through the walk, youth were spiritually moved to offer hope to unchurched children by volunteering their summer and sharing their lives and faith in a summer day camp program for the community.

The Christian faith as taught by the Apostle Paul to the believers in Rome embraced a stance of hope in the midst of trials and challenges:

> Therefore, since we are justified by faith, we have peace with God through our Lord Jesus Christ, through whom we have obtained access to this grace in which we stand; and we boast in our hope of sharing the glory of God. And not only that, but we boast also in our sufferings, knowing that suffering produces endurance, and endurance produces character, and character produces hope, and hope does not disappoint us, because God's love has been poured into our hearts through the Holy Spirit that has been given to us (Romans 5:1-5).

Most persons shy away from the sufferings that Paul notes will eventually issue in a hope that does not disappoint us, secured through the ministry of the Holy Spirit in our hearts and lives. As the Holy Spirit accompanies us, students can be accompanied by teachers in their journeys amid sufferings. The accompanied journey with a teacher over a course of study, outside of expectations, holds the promise of students gaining new perspectives and sharing over time in actions of service that offers hope to themselves and their neighbors.

The promise of accompaniment also includes the opportunity to learn from other participants *if* dialogue is practiced and a faith community is intentionally nurtured in the process. The *if* can present a challenge with increasing diversity in communities and a climate of incivility present in the wider culture that is too often modeled by warring political leaders. Maintaining dialogue, when perspectives widely differ, is a challenge and in my own thirty five years of teaching, resulted just recently in my needing to compose guidelines for graduate classroom interactions as shared below. Andover Newton Theological School is a diverse seminary with students from many theological traditions and denominations. However, these guidelines also apply to a denominational or interdenominational seminary with greater theological consensus and conformity where differences can emerge on a variety of disputed issues. The guidelines are applicable to a wide variety of settings beyond any classroom.

Guidelines for Classroom Communication

Andover Newton is committed as a school to "treat everyone with dignity and respect." As a community that implies the need for open, respectful and tolerant attitudes and an inclusive stance in exploring similarities and differences.

One goal in this course is to understand the *what* and *why* of our own and others' philosophies, theologies and perspectives on religious education. (The *what* and *why* questions are perennial in educational philosophy and human inquiry.)

For peer exchanges in written and oral form we begin with an affirmation or appreciation of what is held in common before exploring differences by posing questions. Any criticism shared needs to be constructive and not from a judgmental stance that dismisses or demeans one's neighbor's position or person. Peer exchanges are an opportunity for mutual ministry, especially at the graduate level.

The statement of one's personal view cannot be a guise for intolerance, disrespect or lack of civility in engaging others. Being open to be challenged by others in the common search for truth across genuine differences is risky, but requires vigilance and diligence in the content and method of our communication.

My suggestions are:
1. Learn about others' perspectives, i.e. read and listen openly to folk who differ from you.
2. Respect positions that differ significantly or slightly from yours.
3. Expect mutual respect in genuine dialogue with a willingness to change your views as "ever new light and truth is shed from God's Word" in our lives and journeys.
4. Recognize that God reserves the right to use and bless persons who widely differ from you and me theologically and philosophically and thank God for that reality.
5. The second of the two great commandments expects us to "love our neighbor as ourselves." (Also see Philippians 2:3-4 in a passage that expects us to imitate Christ's humility in our ministries when conflicts arise and we honor the positions of those who differ from us.)

This classroom ideal for communication in a graduate setting is not deterred in maintaining the place for discipline and structure that assures boundaries for a journey and avoids fruitless diversion and discipline problems in teaching at all levels. Here trust in the experience of the teacher, as an accomplished guide, is a matter for consideration in every phase and form of education. Such trust needs to be earned and nurtured over time. Too many examples in the public media recount the betrayal of trust by educators. Allowing for on-going educational evaluation also supports the hope that things can be improved or radically changed in the future of all teaching ministries when we honestly access what worked and what did not work.[112]

## Hope That Abides

My reflections on faith education represent the hope of a grandfather who longs for a better day for his grandchildren and all grandchildren globally dispelling fears wherever possible. But much more, it represents an abiding assurance of God's active involvement in the human drama from creation to consummation evidenced for Christians in the coming and awaited Second Coming of Jesus the Christ. The writer of First John makes a noteworthy connection: "Beloved, we are God's children now; what we will be has not yet been revealed. What we do know is this: when he is revealed, we will be like him, for we will see him as he is. And all who have this hope in him purify themselves, just as he is pure."

---

[112] For a helpful work on evaluation see Sarah B. Drummond. *Holy Clarity: The Practice of Planning and Evaluation.* Herndon, VA: Alban Institute, 2009.

(1 John 3:2-3) This Jesus has begotten through adoption many children and grandchildren of faith as evidenced in the lives of seminary graduates as one example from my setting of theological education.

One graduate of Andover Newton Theological School historically was Adoniram Judson who labored for many years in Burma, now named Myanmar, and observed "the future is as bright as the promises of God." Over the years a number of Burmese students from Myanmar have attended Andover Newton honoring the legacy of Judson and returning to teach leaders in their own nation despite many threats and challenges in their nation. Those challenges include political repression, economic deprivation, religious persecution, social dislocation and cultural isolation under an oppressive military regime. But those graduates return home with a message of hope grounded in the gospel of Jesus Christ and empowered by the Holy Spirit for a better future for Christians and non-Christians alike who strive for God's purposes in living. The risks they take include the courageous sharing of their ideas for alternatives that currently prevents the public distribution of their theological research. The freedom of speech and expression described in chapter two is a privilege many enjoy that they are not yet fully afforded.

Teaching guided, equipped and empowered by the Holy Spirit honors a freedom for hope to be nurtured where only fear and hopelessness currently persist. The death of Elsa Sanchez who was neighbor and friend of Luis and Danny Cortes did not deter their life commitments in service of the hope (*la esperanza*) that they discovered in the Christian faith that is now shared with many nationally and globally. The promise of a living hope is beautifully described in 1 Peter 1:3-12:

Blessed be the God and Father of our Lord Jesus Christ! By his great mercy he has given us a new birth into a living hope through the resurrection of Jesus Christ from the dead, 4 and into an inheritance that is imperishable, undefiled, and unfading, kept in heaven for you, 5 who are being protected by the power of God through faith for a salvation to be revealed in the last time. In this you rejoice, even if now for a little while you have had to suffer various trails, so that the genuineness of your faith—being more precious than gold that, though perishable, is tested by fire—may be found to result in praise and glory and honor when Jesus Christ is revealed. Although you have not seen him, you love him; and even though you do not see him now, you believe in him and rejoice with an indescribable and glorious joy, for you are receiving the outcome of your faith, the salvation of your souls. Concerning this salvation, the prophets who prophesied of the grace that was to be yours made careful search and inquiry, inquiring about the person and time that the Spirit of Christ within them indicated when it testified in advance of the sufferings destined for Christ and the subsequent glory. It was revealed to them that they were serving not themselves but you, in regard to the things that have now been announced to you through those who brought you good news by the Holy Spirit sent from heaven—things into which angels long to look!

Writing to believers undergoing suffering, the writer of First Peter offers a hope that is not only living (v.3) but also enduring (v.4), sustaining (v.5), and rejoicing (vv.6-9) in the light of the Holy Spirit's provision for our human situation (vv. 11-12) made possible in Jesus Christ. We embrace the future with freedom and a living hope.

CHAPTER 10

# Teaching and Freedom for Joy
Robert W. Pazmiño

Freedom for joy in teaching explores the dimension of joy that was evident in Jesus' ministry and life that is now possible for Christian teachers through the coming of the Holy Spirit at Pentecost (Acts 2:1-13). The Holy Spirit anoints the service of Christian teachers following the exemplar of Jesus and we are "looking to Jesus the pioneer and perfecter of our faith, who for the sake of the *joy* that was set before him endured the cross, disregarding its shame, and has taken his seat at the right hand of the throne of God" (Hebrews 12:2). The dimension of joy and teaching in the name of Jesus is explored in another work with details that are not repeated here.[113] Rather the focus of this chapter is upon the parameters of joy experienced in the service of teaching by considering vocation, avocation and recreation. Freedom for joy is explored in a theological discussion of work and leisure in the work of Miroslav Volf, along with the insights of both Maria Harris and James Loder.

All three of these dimensions of teaching, namely vocation, avocation and recreation call for the invocation of the Spirit to embrace joy so that our joy may be full or complete as Jesus himself promised (John 15:11; 16:24; 17:13). For our joy to be complete Paul suggests for Christians the following: "make my joy complete: be of the same mind, having the same love, being in full accord and of one mind" (Phil 2:2). This unity of love and mind requires the work of the Spirit in the hearts and lives of believers. Before exploring joy in relation to Christian vocation, avocation and recreation, it helps to consider first the nature of joy and its biblical understandings that serve to clarify its significance for teachers and learners in their ministries and everyday lives.

---

[113] Robert W. Pazmiño, *So What Makes Our Teaching Christian?: Teaching in the Name, Spirit and Power of Jesus* (Eugene, Ore.: Wipf and Stock, 2008), 55-63.

## What Is Joy?[114]

Joy is a sense of delight occasioned by God's abiding presence and mediated by the Holy Spirit in all of life that leads to the experience of awe, reverence, and celebration of life as God's gracious gift. This began at the creation and extends to the consummation through the new creation made possible in Jesus Christ. Habakkuk 3:17-19 suggests that joy can transcend the existential human experiences of success, happiness or fruitfulness because of the source being God who abides with believers in all circumstances:

> Though the fig tree does not blossom, and no fruit is on the vines; though the produce of the olive fails and the fields yield no food; though the flock is cut off from the fold and there is no herd in the stalls, yet I will rejoice in the Lord; I will exult in the God of my salvation. God, the Lord, is my strength; he makes my feet like the feet of a deer, and makes me tread upon the heights.

C. S. Lewis in *Surprised By Joy* distinguishes joy from pleasure and happiness in that joy "is never in our power."[115] Joy is a gift from God's Spirit. Joy is discovered in the ordinary relationships and times of life when a person senses their unity with God that touches the heart, soul, mind and strength. Joy embraces the gift of God's goodness of *shalom* with a holistic response of well-being and connection at the depths of one's soul or spirit. Joy includes the mind with an intellectual embrace of God's care, the heart with an affective resting upon God's sustaining love and an intentional/behavioral trust in God's providence and plenitude beyond the circumstances of life. Joy celebrates the wonder of creation and the dignity and worth of persons resting upon God's gracious care. For Christians, the wonder of new creation made possible in Jesus Christ and the ministry of the Spirit deepens the joy experienced this side of heaven.

*The Interpreter's Dictionary of the Bible* notes: "The experience of joy, as related to praise and thanksgiving in public worship, or to the quiet confidence of the individual in God, or to the proclamation of God's saving power, is one of the characteristic elements in religious

---

[114] This section draws and elaborates upon the discussion in Robert W. Pazmiño, *So What Makes Our Teaching Christian?* (Eugene, Ore.: Wipf and Stock, 2008), 55-57.

[115] C. S. Lewis, *Surprised By Joy: The Shape of My Early Life* (New York: Harcourt Brace Jovanovich, 1955), 18,72. I explore joy related to Christian education in Robert W. Pazmiño *Basics of Teaching for Christians* (Eugene, OR: Wipf and Stock, 2002), 97-98 and Robert W. Pazmiño, *God Our Teacher* (Grand Rapids: Baker Academic, 2001), 170-71.

faith as described in the Bible."[116] The one difference between Old Testament and New Testament attitudes toward joy is that the New Testament writers go on to the bold statement of joy in suffering as well in salvation. The Old Testament makes clear that a person's cause for rejoicing is in God and not in oneself (Jer 9:23-24). It is in the New Testament that we find the statement of joy in suffering or in weakness seen in terms of a power of God "made perfect in weakness" (Matt 5:12, 2 Cor 12:9)."[117] Again for Christian teachers, the exemplar for the experience of this joy amid suffering is found in Jesus Christ: "looking to Jesus the pioneer and perfecter of our faith, who for the sake of the joy that was set before him endured the cross, disregarding its shame, and has taken his seat at the right hand of the throne of God." (Hebrews 12:2)

*The New Testament Dictionary of New Testament Theology* notes that joy relates to public occasions of worship and the heart of persons in response to God's help (Ps 13:5). Joy includes an emotion (Ps 16:11); joy in someone or something (2 Sam 1:26; Eccl 11:9); joy in God (Neh 8:10; Ps 33:21); joy in God's word (Jer 15:16; Ps 119:14); joy in keeping the commandments (Ps 119:162); joy in the time of salvation (Isa 35:10). Acts 14:17 speaks of joy in the gifts of nature as being God's gifts in creation. The account of Acts 2:26, 28, in applying Psalms 16:8-11 to the resurrection, speaks of joy in the presence of God. In Revelation 12:12 and 18:20 joy is eschatological rejoicing and is related to a joyous feast hosted by Jesus. Luke's Gospel has joy as one of its basic themes and the Pauline epistles testify to the paradox that Christian joy is to be found in the midst of sadness, affliction and care where it gives proof of its power. Therefore, the source of this joy is beyond earthly, human joy for it is joy in the Lord as explored in Paul's Letter to the Philippians.[118] These various biblical perspectives provide background to explore the joy in teaching as companioned by the Spirit.

## The Spirit As Companion of Teachers[119]

The very Spirit of Christ, the Holy Spirit is the companion of Christian teachers in their ministries. Justo González indicates that "the main character of the Book of Acts is the Holy Spirit."[120] The acts of the first-century followers of Jesus include teaching. The Spirit provides the

---

[116] D. Harvey, "Joy," in *The Interpreter's Dictionary of the Bible*, ed. George A. Buttrick (Nashville: Abingdon, 1962), 1000.
[117] Ibid.
[118] E. Beyreuther and G. Finkenrath, "Joy," in *The New International Dictionary of New Testament Theology*, ed. Colin Brown (Grand Rapids: Zondervan, 1971), 352-61.
[119] See Pazmiño, *So What?*, 60 that is elaborated upon here.
[120] Justo L. González, *Acts: The Gospel of the Spirit* (Maryknoll, N. Y.: Orbis, 2001), 8.

power, presence and creative potential to be a source of joy in sharing new and resurrected life with others through teaching and learning. This makes all the difference, just as the first followers of Jesus experienced in Jerusalem and beyond. They were released from the various prisons and human powers that would forbid their teaching and silence their voices. The Spirit provided a well of joy about which Jesus predicted in his own earthly ministry: "As the scripture has said, 'Out of the believer's heart shall flow rivers of living water.' Now he said this about the Spirit, which believers in him were to receive" (John 7:38-39). The followers of Jesus, as described throughout the Book of Acts, had received the Spirit of whom he spoke at the Pentecostal outpouring (Acts 2:1-4). They experienced an additional filling of the Spirit to accomplish their teaching ministries with boldness (Acts 4:31). The Spirit made all the difference in their teaching ministries and this potential for joy extends to all teachers across the centuries and millennia. This joy is experienced in the areas of vocation, avocation and recreation by Christian teachers today.

## Joy in Vocation

A discussion of vocation is helpfully informed by Miroslav Volf's thinking in his book *Work in the Spirit*.[121] His definition of work is helpful in considering the work and vocation of teaching:

> Work is honest, purposeful and methodologically specified social activity whose primary goal is the creation of products or states of affairs that can satisfy the needs of working individuals or their co-creators, or (if primarily an end in itself) activity that is necessary in order for acting individuals to satisfy their needs apart from the need for the activity itself.[122]

Teaching is work with the intended products of learning and the state of informed character in the case of Christian virtues for students as fashioned by the Spirit. Volf distinguishes work from leisure that is the opposite to work, in that it embraces freedom as compared with the coercion and instrumentality of work. Nevertheless, he suggests paradoxically that work at its best is an exercise of freedom.[123] I would suggest that the work of teaching becomes an exercise of freedom in terms of the use of spiritual gifts, fulfilling one's Christian vocation or

---

[121] Miroslav Volf, *Work in the Spirit* (New York: Oxford University, 1991).
[122] Ibid, 10-11.
[123] Ibid, 11-12.

calling as a teacher. Whereas Volf prefers not to embrace vocation in his exploration of normative categories for work, I think in the case of teaching, vocation provides a generative category for the experience of joy. In other words, once a teacher accepts their calling or vocation to teach, they can intentionally invoke their partnership with the Holy Spirit to fulfill their calling. The teacher's calling includes the responsible stewardship of their spiritual gifts and a daily reliance upon the Spirit's strength, wisdom and joy. This is noted in how the nation of Israel experienced a renewal of teaching and shared life in returning from exile as described in Nehemiah 8. The teachers of the nation, namely Nehemiah, Ezra and the Levites affirmed a lesson applicable across the centuries as recorded in Nehemiah 8:10: "for the joy of the LORD is your strength."

Thomas Green provides a useful categorization of the activities of teaching in formal settings for identifying what specific teaching tasks can be imbued with the Spirit through the intentional invocation on the part of Christian teachers. According to Green:

The logical acts of teaching are:
1. Explaining
2. Concluding
3. Inferring
4. Giving reasons
5. Amassing evidence
6. Demonstrating
7. Defining
8. Comparing
9.

The strategic acts of teaching include:
1. Motivating
2. Counseling
3. Evaluating
4. Planning
5. Encouraging
6. Disciplining
7. Questioning

The institutional acts of teaching are:
Collecting money
Chaperoning
Patrolling the hall
Attending meetings
Taking attendance
Consulting parents (or family members)

Keeping records[124]

A teacher can use their spiritual imagination to envision the Spirit accompanying them in each of these named acts or tasks with a graciousness, wisdom and kindness, along with a willingness to confront destructive patterns and false insights. "Speaking the truth in love" (Eph 4:15) is not an easy task in teaching that calls for courage when resistance to truth is present. For some of these tasks, and eventually all of them over time, teachers can prayerfully request God's wisdom to be made available by the Spirit in order to timely practice teaching in ways that best facilitate learning on the part of our students. The work of the Spirit is crucial in motivating students to be open to any teaching as their spirits are teachable and open to change, and open to a longed for transformation, as hoped for and supported by Christian teachers. The institutional acts named by Green have special application to formal education, but all who teach are challenged to maintain some basic order to facilitate learning while being open to the ardor or passion gifted by the Spirit. Fulfilling the acts of teaching with some measure of success is a source of joy with all of the variables that influence any teaching ministry. The opportunistic quality of teaching requires for the Christian a conscious reliance on the Spirit who is the source of joy over the long haul of any sustained ministry. The vocational practice of teaching in search of joy can embody certain principles.

Volf does helpfully identify three normative principles from the "new creation" to guide economic systems in general, that can be directly applicable to educational systems and the vocation of teaching as well. The "new creation" is his main ethical norm for assessing work and the three principles he names are:

1.  Freedom of individuals
2.  Satisfaction of the basic needs of all people
3.  Protection of nature from irreparable damage[125]

As applied to teaching, the first principle of freedom allows students to reject any teaching that is offered. This freedom recognizes the autonomy of learners and the inherent risks of any teaching effort. This choice can also develop critical and creative reflection on the part of participants who are encouraged to think for themselves. Given the real choice of learners in relation to what is taught, Green identifies teaching as a task or process, and the hoped-for learning as a potential

[124] Thomas Green, *The Activities of Teaching* (New York: McGraw-Hill, 1971), 4.
[125] Volf, 15.

achievement or product that is not at all guaranteed.[126] In other words, any teaching cannot guarantee the hoped-for learning that requires the active cooperation and ownership of participants to be effective and to transfer into their lives. Effectiveness and transfer are sources for joy because this is the intention of teachers, as they share their wisdom and own learning with students.

Volf's second principle of the satisfaction of the basic needs of all people is another potential source of joy for teachers who serve to bring about change and transformation in the lives of people. The mention of "all people" implies for teaching a willingness to vary the teaching approach and method to address the variability of learning styles that exist across any student group. Such styles include visual, auditory, kinesthetic, interactive and other styles such as haptic and olfactory that relate to new research on brain functions and how persons perceive and relate to the world. In addition, the work on multiple intelligences by Howard Gardner identified linguistic, logical-mathematical, spatial, bodily-kinesthetic, musical, interpersonal and intrapersonal intelligences.[127]

Beyond styles and multiple intelligences, some best learn through a low-context teaching setting that focuses on individual learning achievement and a logical and rational sequence of content. Others learn best through a high-context setting that focuses on cooperative and collaborative learning achievement and a psychological and experiential sequence of experiences. In the case of high-context learning preference, social and emotional intelligence is valued to complement a commitment to academic excellence that is of higher value in low-context setting. Cultural differences do influence the preference of low-context or high-context learning. But joy can be experienced in cases where an individual learns both in their preferred style and is also encouraged to be stretched beyond such a preference to gain new insights and experiences. In this case the effort is both to support learners on the one hand with their preferences and to challenge them well beyond their preferences in a holistic approach. Such an approach can result in the joy of learning beyond expectations that is open to new light and truth that the Holy Spirit can bless all persons participating.

Volf's second principle has additional implications beyond individuals and their styles and intelligences, for community. It implies practicing solidarity and a preferential option for the poor and those who have been marginalized in their educational life. Every person is called to

---

[126] Green, 142-143.
[127] Howard Gardner *Frames of Mind: The Theory of Multiple Intelligences* (New York: Basic Books, 1983).

be an heir with Christ in the community of God's people.[128] This wider social perspective follows from the creation and models the triune interdependence found in the perichoretic life of the Trinity.

Volf's third principle, namely protection of nature from irreparable damage applies to teaching with an ecological commitment. In this case, the global ecological crisis looms as all of creation groans for the full liberation described in Romans 8:18-30. The value of Amerindian culture requires teachers and students to consider the legacy left for the seventh generation to come from our choices and ways of living today. In addition, the matter of educational equity emerges given the propensity of human nature to view as deficient any difference discerned in others. Jesus' teaching to love one's neighbor as oneself implies respecting one's neighbor who also bears the image of God and therefore in need of respect and care. When this happens, joy is experienced by all when "the other" becomes a beloved neighbor.

Educational equity can be defined in terms of access to educational resources, respect of difference, space to be heard, the presence of appropriate role models, and shared power and authority at all levels of educational programs in representative proportion.[129] Such a definition of equity is an ideal that calls for the expression of joy and love in the social sphere of our lives. Joy in the social sphere embodies justice along with a concern for righteousness in all human relationships. Loving persons in the public and social sphere requires addressing those conditions that prevent a just and equitable life for all of God's children. Love involves caring enough to confront patterns of exclusion and injustice that historically have plagued educational institutions and structures. The impacts of racism, sexism, classism and other forms of oppression have ravaged the educational opportunities and experiences of far too many persons and groups. The joyful and loving response to these realities calls for seeing that one of the tasks of teaching is to confront the destroyers of life. These destroyers are manifest in different forms that call for spiritual engagement to make a concrete difference for the "common good" (1 Cor 12:7). Teachers are called to love and care enough to speak up and act on behalf of that common good.

## Joy in a Vocation

All that has been discussed in vocation above can apply to those whose primary work or ministry is not formal teaching, but who

---

[128] Volf, 16.
[129] Robert W. Pazmiño, *Latin American Journey: Insights for Christian Education in North America* (Cleveland: United Church Press, 1994), 84, 117.

nevertheless exercise anointed gifts of teaching in their capacity as volunteers in diverse ministries on a weekly, daily or more sporadic basis. For them, teaching assumes the status of being an amateur. The root of the word "amateur" is worth consideration because as a French word it derives from the Latin *amator* or lover, and *amare* or to love. Therefore, as an amateur one engages in teaching out of sheer love and for the sheer joy it involves in the expression of that love. This is in keeping with the exemplar of Jesus as we are "looking to Jesus the pioneer and perfecter of our faith, who for the sake of the joy that was set before him endured the cross, disregarding its shame, and has taken his seat at the right hand of the throne of God" (Hebrews 12:2). The cross for the amateur teacher can include the real costs of time, energy and commitment in the exercise of their spiritual gift.

Many volunteer teachers assume a major commitment in agreeing to teach and take seriously the time required to faithfully teach, sharing their lives in relationships along with their particular teaching content with their students. I recall that while working fulltime as a crisis counselor for emotionally disturbed children and their families in a psychiatric setting and being a young father of a preschooler in our family, I volunteered to both teach a weekly Sunday school class for youth each Sunday and to be one of the adult leaders for the youth and young adult group that met every Friday night at church. The Friday night commitment involved leading an inductive Bible study with twelve to fifteen youth from 7 to 8 pm followed by a teaching segment for the gathered youth fellowship on numerous topics selected by the youth officers using a survey of all the members. The best attended sessions included the topics "Sex is not a four-letter word" and "Communication with parents in difficult times."

After forty years, I recall the joy in preparing and the actual teaching times where youth spiritually grew in significant ways. As a result of this ministry, faithfully undergirded by the prayers of elders in the church known as prayer warriors, a number of the youth eventually entered various fulltime ministries in churches and community organizations. The joy of this service finds expression in the transformed lives of students who in turn have faithfully taught others fulfilling the pattern the Apostle Paul commended to Timothy in 2 Timothy 2:2: "and what you have heard from me through many witnesses entrust to faithful people who will be able to teach others as well." The freedom for joy was realized through the forms of disciplined study and a willingness to share one's life along with one's teaching in this ministry (1 Thes 2:8; 1 Tim 4:16). The invocation of the Spirit in the avocation of teaching requires a devotion, dedication and commitment exemplified historically in the ministry of Ezra: "For Ezra had set his heart to study the law of the LORD, and to do it, and to teach the statutes and ordinances in Israel" (Ezra 7:10). Teaching as a form of Christian work "must be done under the inspiration of the Spirit and in the light of the new creation."[130] Teachers can say, "I work and the Spirit of the resurrected Christ works through me," for the Spirit works with the rule of love that an amateur teacher in essence embraces.[131]

## Joy in Recreation

Volf in his discussion of work contrasts it from leisure that can be equated with my consideration of recreation here. The Holy Spirit is the *spiritus creator* who actively blesses all of life to bring renewal and refreshment. Volf defines his use of leisure:

> Leisure is an activity that is primarily an end in itself and hence (as activity) satisfies a need for acting individuals, but is at the same time not necessarily for, or done with the primary goal of, meeting other needs, either of the acting individuals themselves or their fellow creatures. Work and leisure are not mutually exclusive, and are opposite poles on a continuum.[132]

Volf continues:

> Enjoyment of the beauty of nature, delight in exercise and development of one's own skills, and appreciation of fellowship with one another are three fundamental aspects of leisure activity.[133]

By affirming the goodness of creation, biblical faith encourages ones enjoyment of it.[134] The Spirit's presence in all of life beyond what is commonly understood as teaching work or voluntary service in teaching, embraces that the chief end of persons is the glorification and enjoyment of God. That glorification and enjoyment includes the blessings of creation evident in nature and in the human community. All good gifts in life are gracious offerings of God adding joy to everyday life. "The most fundamental of all human needs is the need for communion with God. Mary, who sat at the Lord's feet and listened to his teaching, had chosen 'the most needful thing.'" (Luke 10:42)[135] The enjoyment of God finds

---

[130] Volf, 79.
[131] Ibid, 115.
[132] Ibid, 133-134.
[133] Ibid, 136.
[134] Ibid, 151.
[135] Ibid, 152.

its fullest expression in the freedom of worship discussed in chapter three. But joy is discovered in the various teachable moments that accompany everyday life via times of recreation and leisure. Joyful glimpses of God can often accompany the relaxed walk or even the troubled walk as in the case of the disciples on the road to Emmaus (Luke 24:13-35) where Jesus posed questions and sensitively listened before opening the scriptures. This teaching event was extended to share fellowship over a meal when Jesus' disciples experienced joy in the breaking of bread together (Luke 24:28-35). "The Spirit inspires and gifts people not only to work, but also to enjoy 'festive companionship' with God."[136]

Recreation by the Spirit is possible in a vast host of activities and in-activities. In-activities honor the need for Sabbath and can include encounters with nature, music and the arts or just mindful breathing, seeing and listening in everyday life. These activities and in-activities relate to teaching and become a source of joy when they are shared with others and invite reflection upon the presence of God. Singing, meditation, prayer, writing and imaginative play are some examples that come to mind and even reading as opportunities to re-create our awareness of the gift of joy God intends for God's beloved children in this world and the next. The arts honor this dimension of our created lives where God delights and invites us to be co-creators and to experience the joy lavishly shared upon all of creation. Here are sources of joy to gladden the hearts and spirits of teachers who are often reminded only with their time shared with children. A question I often pose in settings where teachers are gathered is: Where is the joy? It is a question that can invite and ignite the search for joy as gifted by the Spirit for each day of our lives while practicing the presence of God.

---

[136] Ibid, 137.

PART THREE

# Teaching in The Spirit and Sustenance

Education that liberates and education that celebrates are timely challenges because Christians recognize that God sustains us as he did Jacob during his journey in the desert. In returning to the Song of Moses, Deuteronomy 32:10 describes this to be the case: "God sustained him in a desert land, in a howling wilderness waste; he shielded him, cared for him, guarded him as the apple of his eye." This was also the case for both Hagar and Ishmael who were both dispelled from Abraham's household given the protests of Sarah. Through institutional, communal, national, global, familial and personal challenges, God presence through the ministry of the Holy Spirit sustains us in our teaching and learning.

The Song of Moses from Deuteronomy 32, noted earlier, is also mentioned in Revelation 15:3-4. As K. H. Bartels notes "the other song of Moses in the Old Testament is found in Exodus 15:1-18 where Moses and the Israelites celebrated the deliverance from Pharaoh's army and the liberation of the people. The writer of Revelation, John, transposes the song of Moses in Exodus 15 and also includes words from Psalm 145:7 giving them a Christological significance."[137] Psalm 145 celebrates the greatness and goodness of God and verse 7 reads: "They shall celebrate the fame of your abundant goodness, and shall sing aloud of your righteousness."

Returning to Revelation 15: 3-4, we read: "And they (referring to the seven angels) sing the song of Moses, the servant of God, and the song of the Lamb:

Here is the "Song of the Lamb:"
Great and amazing are your deeds, Lord God the Almighty!
Just and true are your ways, King of the nations!
Lord, who will not fear and glorify your name?
For you alone are holy.

---

[137] Bartels, p. 674

All nations will come and worship before you,
for your judgments have been revealed.

This glorious Song of the Lamb celebrates what the Second Moses, our Lord Jesus Christ accomplished and all we need to communicate through our teaching ministries to a world with great spiritual need and hunger. The dynamic relationship between the Songs of Moses is linked by the writer of Revelation to the consummation of all creation. Hannah's prayer and Mary's Magnificat echo these very same themes.

In returning to Deuteronomy 32:5-14, we discover that all is not well with the generations and the Lord's people personified in the person of Jacob and his descendants. But despite it all and despite us, God sustains and cares for those people seeking to follow God's ways. God's care and grace 'despite us' is a message of hope amid God's judgment. God sustains us in our learning and in our teaching throughout our lives as life-long learning is anticipated in Matthew 28:18-20 along with Jesus' promise to be with us always. Blessings along with warnings are issued to God's people in our earthly journeys. Exodus 16:32 records that God asked Moses to store up two quarts of manna because God wanted future generations to see the food that sustained folk in the desert. In verse 33 of that chapter Moses told Aaron: "Put some manna in a jar and store it in the place of worship for future generations to see." The Spirit's daily sustenance is manna for Christian teachers wandering in the wilderness of educational fads and changes in the third millennium.

Teaching can be inherently a hopeful venture for it assumes and proposes that some folk are gathered together and capable of learning. It also suggests that the teachers or students have something of value to share. In the case of Christian faith, teaching affirms the belief that God is our Teacher. God was the teacher of Abraham, Isaac and Jacob; and God was the teacher of Sarah, Rebekah, Leah and Rachel. God has been the teacher of our lives from the very knitting together of our bodies in our mother's womb as beautifully described in Psalm 139:13-16, from our passing through birth into this world, and from the journeys of our lives to this very point today. Do we sense and appreciate the wonder of that gift of God's sustaining presence and teaching in all of life? What hope can we bring to our lives and the lives of others even in a time of global economic crisis or recession and national challenge?

Teaching that sustains us involves both denunciation and annunciation. Our life is sustained by our breathing each moment and we are to be conscious of the Lord, Giver of Life, sustaining our breath each day as a gift. With breath there is life, and without it death. My wife's recent struggle with COP (Cryptogenic Organizing Pneumonitis) for over a year has made me very conscious of the importance of breathing for our life. With the denunciation of the destroyers of life comes the possibility of announcing the new life God is bringing into our lives. The New Testament pattern is life, death and new life in Jesus Christ and in the coming of the Holy Spirit at Pentecost. Gabriel Moran in his work *Showing How: The Act of Teaching* suggests that to teach is to show how to live and how to die.[138] I would add, to teach is to show how to love and how to live again. To live again is to live anew through God's gracious transformation and renewal gifted to us by God's Spirit, the Spirit of Jesus, the Blessed Holy Spirit who anoints our teaching ministries. This is our Pentecostal identity and calling.

Anointed teaching sustains persons, communities, societies and all of creation that is hankering and groaning for new life. As described in the Book of Acts, all of Jesus' disciples turned their first century world upside down; so we are invited to do the same today. Anointed teaching fosters the love of God, neighbor, self and all of creation. One of the memory verses from my Sunday School years as a child was of course John 3:16, "For God so loved the world, that he gave his only begotten Son, that whosoever believeth in him should not perish, but have everlasting life." God's love of the world and all of creation found expression in the remarkable gift of Jesus (2 Cor 9:15), God's Son and the gift of everlasting life for all who believe in him. Speaking of memory verses, when I was left to my own choices and devices for verse selection I searched the Bible and discovered: John 11:35 "Jesus wept;" 1 Thes 5:16 "Rejoice evermore;" and I Thes 5:17 "Pray without ceasing." You can imagine my joyful surprise to find two adjacent short verses in 1 Thessalonians 5 after my long biblical search for short memory verses!

Teaching in the name of Jesus can offer an alternative and foster a sense of hope for persons, families, groups and communities. The Apostle Paul in his letter to the Ephesians described the experiences of persons before coming to faith in Jesus Christ as "having no hope and without God in the world." (Eph 2:12) In his work *Race Matters*, Cornel West advocates for a politics of conversion that provides "a chance for people to believe there is hope for the future and a meaning to struggle" that Christian faith provides.[139] His politics apply not just to African Americans, but all folk globally who hunger for freedom, liberation and a new life. Those on the margins of society, those identified as the *anawim*,

---

[138] Gabriel Moran, *Showing How: The Act of Teaching* (Valley Forge, PA: Trinity Press International, 1997), 39.
[139] Cornel West, *Race Matters* (Boston: Beacon Press, 1993), 18.

particularly hunger for an alternative life.[140] It was the *anawim* to whom Jesus paid particular attention in his teaching ministry. As Christian teachers we can ask ourselves two questions: Who are those who feel life is hopeless? How are Christians making a difference with those persons?

It is noteworthy that the communal life is discussed before personal life because of the priority the community holds over individuals. Understanding God as a communion of three persons is a theological warrant for considering communities and families of faith before individuals and to counter the narcissistic aspects of contemporary culture. Starting with "Teaching and Communal Life" in chapter eleven can potentially nurture a shift to a "we-generation" of Jesus' followers instead of the "me-generation" that persists in the wider global culture.

---

[140]Robert W. Pazmiño, *By What Authority Do We Teach?* (Grand Rapids: Baker Books, 1994), 63-65, 69, 77, 99, 144.

CHAPTER 11

# Teaching and Communal Life
Robert W. Pazmiño

Hispanic theologian Samuel Solivan observes "it is the person and work of the Holy Spirit that enables human and social transformation."[141] He cites an essential affirmation of the Spirit's personhood as articulated by Thomas Oden:

Like a person, the Spirit can be resisted (Acts 7:51), avoided, or responsively answered (Acts: 10:19-21). Only a person can be vexed (Isa. 63:10) or grieved (Ephes. 4:30). Only one with intelligence and the capacity for communication can speak from heart to heart. These are qualities of personhood. Only a person can teach, talk, reveal his will to other persons, become angry (Isa. 63:10). As persons speak and communicate, so does the Holy Spirit speak in Scripture to the faithful (Mark 13:11; Acts 8:29; 21:11; 1 Tim. 4:1; Rev. 2:7) to disclose his will and listen responsively to creatures.[142]

The personhood of the Spirit from the beginning of created time supports the value, dignity and personhood of all people. God as triune embodied the personal and communal nature of reality. God is a community of what biblically is named Father, Son and Spirit. Humans are created in God's image and humanity reflects this communal dimension of life. Human personhood is realized in the intimate connections that persons have in their families, local communities and a host of social connections that comprise everyday life. We become persons by virtue of the relationships that have sustained us from the beginning of life. Birth emerging from within our mothers' wombs or even by artificial insemination assumes human connection and human agency within diverse communities. The genetic material passed on to persons at birth is a legacy from ancestors within the families of our

---

[141] Samuel Solivan, "The Holy Spirit: A Pentecostal Hispanic Perspective," in *Teología en Conjunto:A Collaborative Hispanic Protestant Theology* (Louisville: Westminster/John Knox, 1997), 54.
[142] Thomas C. Oden, *Life in the Spirit: Systematic Theology,* Vol. 3 (San Francisco: Harper Collins, 1992), 20, as noted in Solivan, 54.

origins. In addition, the culture and language taught to us is the product of human communities.

## Education and Its Role in Communities

Education itself can be defined as "the entire process by which a culture transmits itself across the generations."[143] Beyond this definition, Jerome Bruner suggests that education is "not only a process that transmits culture but also one that provides alternative views of the world and strengthens the will to explore them."[144] The great axles of "American" (referring to the United States, but applicable to all of the Americas) society in the colonial period (1607-1783) according to Bernard Bailyn were the family, congregation, community and economy.[145] Later in the history of the United States other axles that emerged were schools, child-care and youth agencies, the media of various forms and the body politic itself that shaped and determined educational policies and practices. Communal life as generally understood encompassed families, congregations, local schools and neighborhoods including peers and those agencies that offered programs for the care of children and youth in their formative years at the local level. Each person has an educational configuration or ecology of influences from these communal and corporate entities that serve to shape them and to pass on knowledge, values, attitudes, skills and sensitivities for how life is viewed and lived.[146]

Each and every person has a communal matrix in which they live, move and have their being and the Christian faith affirms that it is in God "we live and move and have our being" (Acts 17:28) as the Apostle Paul suggested to the Greeks quoting one of their poets in first-century Athens. God intends a replication of the shared life enjoyed within the Trinity (*perichoresis*) for the experience of persons in human communities. The task before Christian teachers is therefore to make explicit and implicit connections between God and the matrix of communal life with the intent of sharing information, fostering formation and inviting transformation in partnership with the person and work of the Holy Spirit. Spiritual imagination encourages the exploration and implementation of alternatives to current realities. This is a life-long task

---

[143] Bernard Bailyn, *Education in the Forming of American Society* (New York: W. W. Norton, 1960), 14.

[144] Jerome S. Bruner, *On Knowing: Essays for the Left Hand* (New York: Antheneum, 1962), 117.

[145] Bailyn, 45.

[146] Lawrence A. Cremin, *Traditions of American Education* (New York: Basic Books, 1977), 134.

as suggested by the educational commission Jesus shared with his followers at the close of Matthew's Gospel (Matt 28:18-20).

## New Testament Communal Roots: Matthew and Romans

It is noteworthy that Matthew appears as the first of the Gospels in the New Testament though scholars generally agree that it was not the first Gospel written historically. Mark's Gospel holds that distinction. Why then does Matthew's Gospel appear first? One colleague, who taught New Testament, William Herzog, suggested that Matthew was an essential catechetical document intended to be taught to followers of Jesus. The structure of the Gospel itself organizes Jesus' teaching into five blocks or units modeling the Pentateuch and concludes with Jesus' challenging words to his disciples at its conclusion:

> All authority in heaven and earth has been given to me. Go therefore and make disciples of all nations, baptizing them in the name of the Father and of the Son and of the Holy Spirit, and teaching them to obey everything that I have commanded you. And remember, I am with you always, to the end of the age. (Matt 28:18-20)

This comprehensive commission in the name of the Father, Son and Holy Spirit requires that attention be given to the communal dimensions of faith life.

The Trinity itself is a community of three intimately related persons suggested by the theological concept of *perichoresis* or shared life. "*Perichoresis* implies a joint and interdependent life that requires a transformation of the human heart to embrace the human community."[147] This transformation is possible through the work of the Holy Spirit in the teaching ministries of Christian communities. Followers of Jesus are to be taught *everything* that Jesus himself commanded as a component of their shared life in the Christian community. This task requires life-long education in the process of making disciples and requires daily reliance upon a partnership with the Holy Spirit who is the agent by which Jesus remains with us to the end of the age. Remembering itself is a responsibility requiring a daily anointing with God's Spirit and the making of disciples requires the work on the Holy Spirit in the hearts of students. Human and social transformation that is genuine and sustainable is only possible as the Holy Spirit moves across the teaching and learning efforts in communal life to accomplish God's purposes.

---

[147] Robert W. Pazmiño, *God Our Teacher: Theological Basics in Christian Education* (Grand Rapids: Baker Academic, 2001, 31.

James Loder was known to have a theological dictum that was shared with his students in relation to Christian education that flows from Matthew's educational commission: "It takes the Trinity to raise a child."[148]

To expand upon Loder's insights I would suggest: It takes a faithful congregation or faith community to raise a child. In addition to the key role that families play, faith communities are essential to the faith formation of children, youth and adults. Congregants work in partnership with the Holy Spirit to pass on to Jesus' disciples all that Jesus taught to obey in following his commandments. The summary of his commandments is found in the Two Great Commandments of loving God and one's neighbors (Matt. 22:37-40). In a time of global ecological crisis, I would add the need to love God's creation that is itself the object of God's love and care as suggested in John 3:16: "For God so loved *the world* that he gave his only Son, so that everyone who believes in him may not perish but have eternal life." God's plans to bless humanity in the sending of Jesus are extended to include all of creation as Romans 8: 18-30 explicitly teaches:

> I consider that the sufferings of this present time are not worth comparing with the glory about to be revealed to us. ¹For the creation waits with eager longing for the revealing of the children of God; for the creation was subjected to futility, not of its own will but by the will of the one who subjected it, in hope that the creation itself will be set free from its bondage to decay and will obtain the freedom of the glory of the children of God. We know that the whole creation has been groaning in labor pains until now; and not only the creation, but we ourselves, who have the first fruits of the Spirit, groan inwardly while we wait for adoption, the redemption of our bodies. For in hope we were saved. Now hope that is seen is not hope. For who hopes for what is seen? But if we hope for what we do not see, we wait for it with patience.
>
> Likewise the Spirit helps us in our weakness; for we do not know how to pray as we ought, but that very Spirit intercedes with sighs too deep for words. And God, who searches the heart, knows what is the mind of the Spirit, because the Spirit intercedes for the saints according to the will of God.
>
> We know that all things work together for good for those who love God, who are called according to his purpose. For those whom he foreknew he also predestined to be conformed to the image of his Son, in order that he might be the firstborn within a large family. And those

---

[148] James Loder's words as cited by Dana R. Wright "The Potential Contribution of Loder to Practical Theological Science," in *Redemptive Transformation in Practical Theology* eds. Dana R. Wright and John D. Kuentzel (Grand Rapids: Eerdmans, 2004), 426.

whom he predestined he also called; and those whom he called he also justified; and those whom he justified he also glorified.

The communal dimension of God's plan for the children of God are universal in scope and require recognition of the first and ultimate fruits of the Spirit that brings freedom to persons and all of creation. The intercessory prayer of the Spirit is essential in the process and the emergence of a "large family" of folk who love God. A glimpse of what God purposes for the faith community is found in an Old Testament example of communal teaching.

## Communal Teaching: One Old Testament Example

A remarkable description of the renewal brought to the faith community through faithful teaching is found in Nehemiah 8. This passage, worth quoting at length, captures the teaching ministries of Ezra, the Levites, and all the people in their mourning and celebration that shaped the communal life of the nation returning from exile and rebuilding Jerusalem:

All the people gathered together into the square before the Water Gate. They told the scribe Ezra to bring the book of the law of Moses, which the LORD had given to Israel. Accordingly, the priest Ezra brought the law before the assembly, both men and women and all who could hear with understanding. This was on the first day of the seventh month. He read from it facing the square before the Water Gate from early morning until midday, in the presence of the men and the women and those who could understand; and the ears of all the people were attentive to the book of the law. The scribe Ezra stood on a wooden platform that had been made for the purpose; and beside him stood Mattithiah, Shema, Anaiah, Uriah, Hilkiah, and Maaseiah on his right hand; and Pedaiah, Mishael, Malchijah, Hashum, Hash-baddanah, Zechariah, and Meshullam on his left hand. And Ezra opened the book in the sight of all the people, for he was standing above all the people; and when he opened it, all the people stood up. Then Ezra blessed the LORD, the great God, and all the people answered, "Amen, Amen," lifting up their hands. Then they bowed their heads and worshiped the LORD with their faces to the ground. Also Jeshua, Bani, Sherebiah, Jamin, Akkub, Shabbethai, Hodiah, Maaseiah, Kelita, Azariah, Jozabad, Hanan, Pelaiah, the Levites, helped the people to understand the law, while the people remained in their places. So they read from the book, from the law of God, with interpretation. They gave the sense, so that the people understood the reading.

And Nehemiah, who was the governor, and Ezra the priest and scribe, and the Levites who taught the people said to all the people,

"This day is holy to the LORD your God; do not mourn or weep." For all the people wept when they heard the words of the law. Then he said to them, "Go your way, eat the fat and drink sweet wine and send portions of them to those for whom nothing is prepared, for this day is holy to our LORD; and do not be grieved, for the joy of the LORD is your strength." So the Levites stilled all the people, saying, "Be quiet, for this day is holy; do not be grieved." And all the people went their way to eat and drink and to send portions and to make great rejoicing, because they had understood the words that were declared to them.

On the second day the heads of ancestral houses of all the people, with the priests and the Levites, came together to the scribe Ezra in order to study the words of the law. And they found it written in the law, which the LORD had commanded by Moses, that the people of Israel should live in booths during the festival of the seventh month, and that they should publish and proclaim in all their towns and in Jerusalem as follows, "Go out to the hills and bring branches of olive, wild olive, myrtle, palm, and other leafy trees to make booths, as it is written." So the people went out and brought them, and made booths for themselves, each on the roofs of their houses, and in their courts and in the courts of the house of God, and in the square at the Water Gate and in the square at the Gate of Ephraim. And all the assembly of those who had returned from the captivity made booths and lived in them; for from the days of Jeshua son of Nun to that day the people of Israel had not done so. And there was very great rejoicing. And day by day, from the first day to the last day, he read from the book of the law of God. They kept the festival seven days; and on the eighth day there was a solemn assembly, according to the ordinance.

Worship is central in this account of communal renewal along with the key role of interpretation provided by those who taught the people. Worship enables experiencing the joy of the Lord and great rejoicing contributes to the formation and strength of the community. Though implicit in this Nehemiah passage, the Spirit is working in the faith community through the lives and ministries of all participants. The ministry of Ezra, who proclaims the word of God before all those who could understand it, is noteworthy as the first mention of a pulpit in the biblical record. Ezra as the leader was exemplary in his ministry as one who had "set his heart to study the law of the Lord, and to do it, and to teach the statutes and ordinances in Israel." (Ezra 7:10) In this passage, the educational work of the Levites is described where they work in small groups of persons to foster the understanding of the scriptures that Ezra shared. The Levites as distinct from the temple priests, who provided oversight for the religious ritual, were the teaching priests who helped learners appropriate the significance of biblical insights for living together in community.[149]

The leaders of the returning community studied together the words of the law that assisted them to work in unity and peace. It is noteworthy that the response of the people includes the sending of portions to those for whom nothing is prepared to eat. One can imagine how the making of booths and living in them together was an important element for the excitement and participation of the children and youth in the community, as well as adults in their intergenerational contacts. The Festival of Booths with its elaborated and embodied worship sustained the community over a period of eight days that would have allowed for significant time for informal and nonformal education as persons lived together in temporary shelters, reminding them of their ancestors' and their own sojourn. One can also imagine stories recounted of the nation's past and its significance for then contemporary life and its common problems. Such occasions serve to form the identity of a community and to enliven the connections for mutual support and resourcing across the generations. They also serve to challenge the community for next steps to take in its call for a growing faithfulness to God in their corporate life all guided by the God's Spirit.

Transitions in the life of the faith community require taking stock and reflecting on the past to discern the ways in which God has provided for the people. Such knowledge invites a continuing trust in God and a renewed reliance upon the leaders God has provided for the ongoing life of the community. Covenants previously formed need to be revisited and renewed in order to journey forward. A covenantal renewal is an opportunity for lament, confession, praise, adoration, and joy shared in worship. Looking back involves lament and confession for what was not accomplished and what occasioned the exile in Babylon. But despite these failures, God's forgiveness, forbearance, mercy and steadfast love sustained the people enabling the return to Jerusalem. Such love and mercy warrant the praise, adoration and thanksgiving of the leaders and people alike recognizing God's mighty acts on behalf of the nation and God's invitation to a new beginning. As a result, the people can hear and embrace the lived reality shared by their leadership: "the joy of the Lord is your strength" (Neh 8:10).

God's Spirit worked in the lives of the leadership and people alike to reshape the community upon its return from exile. The Spirit providentially worked in the hearts and lives of both Nehemiah and Ezra

---

[149] For a full discussion of this passage and its educational implications, see Robert W. Pazmiño, *Latin American Journey: Insights for Christian Education in North America* (Cleveland: United Church Press, 1994), reprint ed. (Eugene, OR: Wipf and Stock, 2002), 123-144.

prior to their actual return to shape their desires (Psalm 37:4) and in the shaping of their spiritual gifts, all required to lead the nation. In addition, the teaching corps of the Levites was also drawn by the Spirit to consider and then undertake the journey and transition back to their homeland. Those people who elected to return were also led and quickened by the Spirit rather than remaining in Babylon. Real costs were assumed in opting for the return, but also potential blessings including freedom with all of its liabilities and responsibilities in a new and formidable setting. One can imagine the choices were not in every case easy, but required a counting of the costs and a willingness to venture in the company of others. That venture included the formation of a new gathered community led by God's Spirit while confronting numerous threats and risks. All those risks were undergirded by the accompaniment of God's Spirit along the way and in each step as the new community faced opposition of various forms.

From the description of the Nehemiah 8 account above, the communal purposes or tasks of worship and community formation stand out. These are two of the five tasks that I have discussed as emerging from the biblical foundations of Christian education that require the exercise of spiritual gifts to sustain a community and to nurture its common good.[150] The additional three tasks are service, advocacy and proclamation that are equally present in this passage and deserving of attention.

The Spirit enabled the proclamation of God's Word that launched the gathering of the community as Ezra proclaimed the scripture for all to understand. The complementary teaching ministry of the Levites is noted. They fostered understanding that was facilitated by dividing the large congregation into smaller groups where discussion, dialogue and questions were more readily possible. Service is evident in the sharing of food with those who did not have provision and in the preparation of the food itself that unnamed folk accomplished. The construction of the booths was another service evident and the inevitable cleanup after the festival. Advocacy is implicit in the remembrance of those who had no food and the potential on the part of the heads of the ancestral homes who may have identified those remaining on the margins of the community needing a voice. As a result of the meeting of leaders, news did spread to all their towns about the upcoming festival inviting all to participate. Advocacy can result in wider inclusion for those who too readily are forgotten when decisions are made. Who is at the table when

---

[150] Robert W. Pazmiño, *Foundational Issues in Christian Education* Third ed. (Grand Rapids: Baker Academic, 2008), 46-55.

decisions are made, and who remains under the table is a matter of justice and equity in the life of communities. In such decisions, the underlying question is what makes a community?

## What Makes a Community?

The religious educator John Westerhoff considered this question that calls for discernment regarding how the Spirit is at work in communal life. The identification and embrace of the common good cemented by those things held in common are essential. Westerhoff proposed that a community of faith has the following elements that are held in common or shared:

1.  A strong sense of identity and openness to the world
2.  A common memory or sharing story
3.  A common vision of goals (ends) and means (norms) for which and by which it lives
4.  A common authority or principle for resolving conflicts between the community's understandings and ways and the situations confronting individuals
5.  Shared life together similar to that of a "family"[151]

To "shared life," common rituals can be added that serve to provide symbolic and aesthetic bonds for community members to embrace. I would also note that common authorities can be plural requiring negotiation regarding priorities in particular contexts and shifting times. The Spirit's ministry is evident in the life of the leadership and all participants as was the case in the Nehemiah passage, where the coordination and complementarity of roles and gifts were essential for community's life together. The Apostle Paul grasps the significance of this interplay of spiritual gifts in his description of how they function under the leadership of the Holy Spirit:

> Now concerning spiritual gifts, brothers and sisters, I do not want you to be uninformed. You know that when you were pagans, you were enticed and led astray to idols that could not speak. Therefore I want you to understand that no one speaking by the Spirit of God ever says "Let Jesus be cursed!" and no one can say "Jesus is Lord" except by the Holy Spirit.
> Now there are varieties of gifts, but the same Spirit; and there are varieties of services, but the same Lord; and there are varieties of

---

[151]John H. Westerhoff, III, "The Future" in John H. Westerhoff, III and O. C. Edwards, eds. *A Faithful Church: Issues in the History of Catechesis* (Wilton, Conn.: Morehouse-Barlow), 302.

activities, but it is the same God who activates all of them in everyone. To each is given the manifestation of the Spirit for the common good. To one is given through the Spirit the utterance of wisdom, and to another the utterance of knowledge according to the same Spirit, to another faith by the same Spirit, to another gifts of healing by the one Spirit, to another the working of miracles, to another prophecy, to another the discernment of spirits, to another various kinds of tongues, to another the interpretation of tongues. All these are activated by one and the same Spirit, who allots to each one individually just as the Spirit chooses.

For just as the body is one and has many members, and all the members of the body, though many, are one body, so it is with Christ. For in the one Spirit we were all baptized into one body—Jews or Greeks, slaves or free—and we were all made to drink of one Spirit.

Indeed, the body does not consist of one member but of many. If the foot would say, "Because I am not a hand, I do not belong to the body," that would not make it any less a part of the body. And if the ear would say, "Because I am not an eye, I do not belong to the body," that would not make it any less a part of the body. If the whole body were an eye, where would the hearing be? If the whole body were hearing, where would the sense of smell be? But as it is, God arranged the members in the body, each one of them, as he chose. If all were a single member, where would the body be? As it is, there are many members, yet one body. The eye cannot say to the hand, "I have no need of you," nor again the head to the feet, "I have no need of you." On the contrary, the members of the body that seem to be weaker are indispensable, and those members of the body that we think less honorable we clothe with greater honor, and our less respectable members are treated with greater respect; whereas our more respectable members do not need this. But God has so arranged the body, giving the greater honor to the inferior member, that there may be no dissension within the body, but the members may have the same care for one another. If one member suffers, all suffer together with it; if one member is honored, all rejoice together with it.

Now you are the body of Christ and individually members of it. And God has appointed in the church first apostles, second prophets, third teachers; then deeds of power, then gifts of healing, forms of assistance, forms of leadership, various kinds of tongues. Are all apostles? Are all prophets? Are all teachers? Do all work miracles? Do all possess gifts of healing? Do all speak in tongues? Do all interpret? But strive for the greater gifts. And I will show you a still more excellent way. (1 Cor 12)

The ministry of the Holy Spirit orchestrates the various gifts, services and activities of the faith community to make possible its sustained life and growth. Conflicts and questions are anticipated and often inevitable;

the Corinthian setting itself for Paul's letter confirms these realities. The "still more excellent way" is the way of love that is elaborated in the following chapter of First Corinthians and the topic of chapter seven of this work. For community life the wisdom of 1 Peter 4:8 applies and serves to summarize Paul's insights, but voiced by Peter who locked horns with Paul on church matters: "Above all, maintain constant love for one another, for love covers a multitude of sins." The covering of sins does not diminish the demands for justice and the difficult work of peace building in the life of faith communities and wider societal relationships. Justice calls for attention to those who have been sinned against in various communities, and requires the analysis of societal systems and structures in relation to their fruits of both liberation and oppression in the everyday lives of people.

## Questions and Responses for a Christian Community

In her work *The Church as Learning Community* Norma Cook Everist identifies two key questions for a Christian community while confronting diversity in a pluralistic culture: "What is the task of the faith community when we assume that the curriculum is the entirety of the world in which we live? How can we equip each person in the Christian learning community to become a teacher and a learner?"[152] Each faith community wrestles with these questions while recognizing the particulars of their local context. Spiritual discernment is essential in faithfully responding to these questions, relying upon the person and work who the Holy Spirit who partners with human teachers. Julie A. Gorman provides insights for answering Everist's questions through consideration of the key role of small groups in the life of Christian churches.[153] "A small group can be a place to begin to learn caring and to learn how to develop commitment" and trust.[154] That trust includes reliance upon one's partnership with the Spirit in all of life and reliance upon the support of others in an interdependent web of relationships guided by the Christian values of truth, love, faith , hope and joy discussed in Part Two of this work. Beyond the essential ministries of small groups, the entire congregation itself can become a learning community recognizing that learning is "comprehensive, relational and

---

[152]Norma Cook Everist, *The Church as Learning Community: A comprehensive Guide to Christian Education* (Nashville: Abingdon, 2002), 9.

[153] See Julie A. Gorman, *Community that is Christian: A Handbook on Small Groups,* Second ed. (Grand Rapids: Baker Books, 2002).

[154] Ibid, 65.

public."[155] The biblical foundation for this communal reality, Thomas Hawkins finds in Jesus' Farewell Discourse from John's Gospel:

> In his Farewell Discourse, Jesus constitutes his disciples as a new community of learning and teaching that will be guided by the Holy Spirit into a deeper understanding of God's revelation made known in Jesus Christ. "I have said these things to you while I am still with you. But the Advocate, the Holy Spirit, whom the Father will send in my name, will teach you everything, and remind you of all that I have said to you." (John 14:25-26). A little later in the same Farewell Discourse, Jesus promises his disciples that "when the Spirit of truth comes, he will guide you into all the truth" (John 16:13). Jesus' words invite the disciples into a new community characterized by change, growth, learning, and transformation.[156]

The Spirit's role in the new community of Jesus' disciples is indispensable and requires the intentional recognition on the part of Christian leaders and teachers regarding their partnership as they minister within the Christian community. This partnership requires a daily refilling and reliance upon the Spirit's guidance as suggested by the prayer of one key church leader and teacher, Augustine of Hippo:

> Breathe in me O Holy Spirit, that my thoughts may all be holy; Act in me O Holy Spirit, that my work, too, may be holy; Draw my heart O Holy Spirit, that I love but what is holy; Strengthen me O Holy Spirit, to defend all that is holy; Guard me, then, O Holy Spirit, that I always may be holy. Amen.[157]

This prayer is appropriate for all who follow Jesus and share their lives together in the Christian community. Augustine's prayer considers the intellectual, emotional, social, moral, physical, and spiritual dimensions of persons who serve as leaders and followers as well in churches and other ministry settings. These are discussed in the introduction to Part Two of this work and can be envisioned as integrated with the spiritual dimension using the hand model proposed by Ted Ward and described there. The Holy Spirit partners with human spirits to form intergenerational spiritual communities that sustain persons across the life span.

---

[155] Thomas R. Hawkins, *The Learning Congregation: A New Vision of Leadership* (Louisville: Westminster/John Knox, 1997), 39.

[156] Ibid, 14.

[157] Augustine of Hippo. "Prayer for the Indwelling of the Spirit," Patron Saints Index: Augustine of Hippo, www.catholic-forum.com/saints/sainta02.htm.

# CHAPTER 12

# Teaching and Personal Life

Octavio J. Esqueda

The great African theologian, Augustine of Hippo, after his conversion to Christianity described his experience and reflections about his new life in Christ in his *Confessions*. In one of his most famous phrases, Augustine rightly expressed the central purpose of our existence when he addressed God in this way, "Thou hast made us for thyself, O Lord, and our heart is restless until it finds its rest in thee."[158] The French philosopher Blaise Pascal held a similar position stating that the ultimate end of our lives finds its purpose in the sovereign God of the universe, "the infinite abyss can only be filled by an infinite and immutable object, that is to say, only by God himself."[159] In the same way, in the Reformed tradition, the Westminster Shorter Catechism starts with the central declaration that gives meaning to our existence: "What is the chief end of man? Man's chief end is to glorify God, and to enjoy him forever."[160]

Consequently, our lives can only find meaning in the triune God who is the central source of everything we are and do. Our teaching flows from who we are because nobody can give what he does not already possess. In order for our teaching and ministry to have the Holy Spirit's anointing, it becomes essential that our lives are established in the triune God and that we walk in step with the Spirit. Our public ministry always reflects our private lives.

This chapter explores some fundamental spiritual life principles that both teachers and students can follow in order to live with the anointing of the Holy Spirit. Christian teaching represents basically a ministry of grace where the God of the universe decides to collaborate with us through the Holy Spirit. This partnership with the Holy Spirit includes proclaiming the new life God offers in Christ and also denouncing everything that prevents the flourishing of this new life. These are not new principles for our spiritual life, but they are key for all believers

---

[158] Agustín de Hipona, "Augustine's Confessions" (*Confesiones*) (Grand Rapids: Sovereing Grace, 1971),
[159] Blaise Pascal. *Pensées*. Section VII, Morality and Doctrine. 425
[160] Catecismo Menor de Westminster. 1.1

regardless of their time and geographical context. For example, as Christian educators in the twenty first century we can learn about our spiritual life following the advice of the important Spanish Reformer Juan de Valdés.

## Juan de Valdés and Spiritual Life

Juan de Valdés is one of the most important and at the same time less-well-known figures in the Spanish and Italian Reformation. Valdés was born approximately in 1509 in Cuenca, Spain and died in 1541 in Naples, Italy.[161] Juan de Valdés published in 1529 *Diálogo de Doctrina Cristiana* (Dialogue about Christian Doctrine), the first "Protestant" book printed in Spain where he emphasizes the authority of the Scriptures and salvation only by Christ alone.[162] After a short while this book was place in the Inquisition list of forbidden books and Valdés moved to Italy where he became the father of the Italian Reformation.[163]

In 1533, Valdés published in Spanish his *Alfabeto Christiano* (Christian Alphabet) and in 1546 the Italian version was published. In the *Alfabeto*, his second work, Valdés establishes several central principles for the Christian life using the structure of a dialogue between himself and Giulia Gonzaga, a noble woman who had the desire to grown in their Christian faith. This work, even though is little known, gives fundamental guidance for Christian educators and for all believers. At the beginning, Valdés stresses that true happiness for human beings can only be found in the life that God offers to us through Christ: "the happiness of man consists in his knowledge of God and of Christ shown by the light of faith, and in the union of the soul with God through faith, hope, and charity. To this happiness only the true Christian can arrive."[164] Valdés also clarifies that we need to know ourselves in order to be sensitive to God's voice and in this way find the contentment God offers that transcends our present circumstances: "Turn within yourself, open the ears of your soul, so that you may hear the voice of God, and think as a true Christian that in this life you can have no other real contentment and rest, than what will come to you by means of the knowledge of God, through the faith and love of God."[165]

---

[161] José C. Nieto. *El Renacimiento y la otra España: Visión Cultural Sociocultural.* (Geneve: Librairie Droz, 1997), 104
[162] David Estrada Herreo, introducción, p. 8. En Juan de Valdés. *Dialógo de Doctrina.* (Sevilla: Editorial MAD, 2008).
[163] Ibid., 7
[164] Juan de Valdés. *Alfabeto Cristiano.* (London: Bostworth & Harrison, 1861), 20
[165] Ibid., 23

The central theme of Juan de Valdés *Alfabeto Christiano* is a list with central principles for believer's spiritual growth. Valdés made clear that these principles are not firm rules that everybody needs to follow, but rather they are spiritual advice for believers in their walk with Christ. This advice is almost 500 years old, but they continue being relevant at the present time and they remind us how important is our spiritual life so we can then serve others. These are the basic steps that Juan de Valdés suggested to Giulia and that we all can learn from them:

1. The first step is, to know that the way in which you have been walking to the present time cannot conduct you to Christ.
2. The second is, that you hold the resolution to walk by this, which without fail will con duct you to Christ.
3. The third, that you determine to begin to walk by it.
4. The fourth, that you lay aside worldly manners and conversation, which tend to separate you from God, and that you put away all curious speculations.
5. The fifth, that you occupy a portion of every day to enter into a knowledge of the world
6. The sixth, that by means of this knowledge you endeavour to slight and abhor the world.
7. The seventh, that you take a little time every day to enter into a knowledge of yourself.
8. The eighth, that by means of this knowledge you labour to free your heart from your selflove.
9. The ninth, that you take another small portion of time to enter into the knowledge of God, and that you enter by the knowledge of Christ.
10. The tenth, that through this knowledge you enamour yourself with God through the medium of Christ, enamouring yourself in like manner with Christ.
11. The eleventh, that as well by the narratives of the Old Testament as by those of the New, you confirm faith in your soul, as much in belief as in confidence.
12. The twelfth, that in the same way you confirm and strengthen in your soul the expectation of Eternal Life.[166]

With these principles, Juan de Valdés highlights the need that we all have to prioritize our relationship with God in our lives. Personal introspection is important to acknowledge our great need for the Lordship of Christ and the guidance of the Holy Spirit. In the same way, we need to remember that God invites us to freely enjoy his presence in

---

[166] Ibid., 125-126

us. Nothing compares to our relationship with God because everything we do reflects our communion with the Lord. God working in us and through us to benefit other people is the core basis of Christian education.

## Dinner with Jesus

Our relationship with God is essential for our lives and ministries and yet it is common to become so busy working for God that we forget the God we attempt to serve. All believers, but especially leaders and Christian teachers, face the temptation to be concerned primarily about our ministry that we neglect our relationship with God and with others. Sadly, many believers proclaim that Christianity is not a religion, but a personal relationship with God, but they live following religious rules and forget the relationship once they decided to follow Christ. Jesus Christ invites us to delight in his presence and to enjoy an intimate relationship with God through the Holy Spirit.

Jesus words to the church in Laodicea in Revelation 3:20 remain a constant invitation to all of us: "Behold, I stand at the door and knock; if anyone hears My voice and opens the door, I will come in to him and will dine with him, and he with Me." Our God desires that we find delight in his presence and takes the initiative to invite us to the dinner table with him. Pastor and Christian singer Jesús Adrián Romero describes in his book *Cenando con Jesús* (Dinner with Jesus) the importance of the dinner table image to explain the type of relationship God wants to have with us.[167] Dinner meals in biblical times and also in many cultures nowadays represent more than just an occasion to satisfy a physical need. Important dinners require preparation and care to make sure that nothing fails and distract us from enjoying the time with our guests. This kind of meals are celebrated with friends and family and we pay attention to every detail at all times because they represent the deep relational commitment among participants. In fact, during special dinners the after-dinner conversation usually continues for hours because we enjoy the time with our love ones and we focus on them not on the clock or external circumstances. The meal is obviously very important, but the truth is that it becomes secondary to the people we share the meal with and the time we spend together.

Jesús Adrián Romero book *Cenando con Jesús* made a huge impact in my life during a time where I was frustrated because my desire to serve God seemed to be blocked for lack of ministry opportunities. At

---

[167] Jesús Adrián Romero. *Cenando con Jesús*. (Lake Mary, FL: Casa Creación), 2002.

that time, I was about to finish my doctorate, but all doors had unexpectedly closed for the different job possibilities that I had. After coming to the United States and many years of hard work studying my master's at the seminary and doctoral degree at the university, I was about to conclude my academic journey, but the prize to my efforts apparently was vanishing in front of my eyes. I longed for serving God and I always thought that after my academic preparation many ministry doors would open for me.

Nevertheless, when I realized that my sacrifices to serve God at the places I thought were the appropriate ones were being unfruitful, I started to lose heart and feel depressed. I could not understand why God was not blessing my desire to serve him. I was confident that earning a doctorate was the necessary key to teach in many places and I had a hard time trying to comprehend, even though I kept my thoughts to myself without telling others, that God would waste the important contribution I could make to his kingdom.

I was at that time that I read *Cenando con Jesús* and it helped me to remember the importance of my relationship with God. The Lord King of the universe was not waiting for me to finish my studies to finally start expanding his kingdom. My ministry was not the most important thing in my life, but my relationship with God. At the end of the book, Jesús Adrián shares a story that great impacted me and that God used to help me to reorganize my priorities:

One time we had an event in San Salvador with an attendance of around ten thousand people. I came to my hotel room very satisfied with everything that had just happened when the Lord spoke to my heart and asked me this question:
--"Are you willing to leave what you are doing for me?"
I immediately responded:
"Everything I do, I do it for you, Lord."
-- "Are you willing to leave what you are doing for me?" He asked me again.
-- "But there are many people who depend on this ministry. They work full-time, -- "I told Him."
He spoke to my heart again and he asked me the same question. I, then, understood the reason for his demand. God was telling me: "Be careful that what you are doing does not become more important that the relationship you have with me."
God did not want that the source of my joy and fulfillment would be what I was doing, but in my relationship with Him.
I then knelt beside my bed and I told Him. "Lord, if it's your desire, I resign right now to the ministry you game me and go back to do what I used to do." I can say with complete certainty that that what I do it's not

even close in importance to me that my intimacy with the Lord. If I had to leave what I am doing and God's will would be to move to a ranch and shepherd goats, I would gladly do it. Jesus wants that we rejoice in Him and not in the gifts that He has given us."[168]

A few months after I understood the importance of my relationship with God, when I was going through a valley because I was finishing my doctorate, but I was not able to find the job I had anticipated, God opened a door I was not expecting and I became the first Mexican professor in the history of Southwestern Baptist Theological Seminary in Fort Worth, Texas. After teaching there for over seven years, God unexpectedly opened another door and I became the first Mexican professor in the history of Talbot School of Theology at Biola University in La Mirada, California. I have been teaching there for several years now and I have learned to rest in God's direction and to enjoy his presence instead of worrying for my place of service or ministry. In fact, I now know that my identity and satisfaction are not related to my studies or academic position. The prestige of the institution where I work or the academic title of "doctor" are completely irrelevant to my position as God's child.

Our God is inviting us to find delight in his presence. Our life and ministry have our relationship with the triune God as the foundation. Our teaching must flow from our lives in intimate relationship with the Father, the Son, and the Holy Spirit. The position and place of our ministries are completely secondary to our bond with God. Our identity in Christ and the Holy Spirit's presence in us become the essential elements in our teaching ministry.

Jesus invites us to experience a personal and communal relationship with him. Teaching with the Holy Spirit's anointing is a prophetic invitation to seat at the table to dine with Jesus. This offer is open and everyone is welcome. God loves us and he looks for us with open arms desiring that we run to him to find peace.

Nevertheless, we need to acknowledge and communicate that in order to enjoy a relationship with Jesus, is imperative to have a humble and simple heart that recognizes our constant need of God's presence in our lives. Pride usually motivates those who believe that their religious activities will give them a special place at the table with God. Pride, however, is a barrier to even have a seat at the table as Christ's guests.

In Matthew 22:1-14, Jesus compared the kingdom of heaven with a wedding banquet. Again, the Bible stresses the banquet or special dinner

---

[168] Ibid., 173

image to describe the relationship Jesus wants with his followers. In this story, Jesus reminds the religious leaders of his time that God invites all people without exception and that humility is the indispensable dress code to participate at the celebration. In fact, those who believe they are worthy to be there or who minimize the invitation will not have a seat at the table.

> Jesus spoke to them again in parables, saying, "The kingdom of heaven may be compared to a king who gave a wedding feast for his son. And he sent out his slaves to call those who had been invited to the wedding feast, and they were unwilling to come. Again he sent out other slaves saying, 'Tell those who have been invited, "Behold, I have prepared my dinner; my oxen and my fattened livestock are *all* butchered and everything is ready; come to the wedding feast."' But they paid no attention and went their way, one to his own farm, another to his business, and the rest seized his slaves and mistreated them and killed them. But the king was enraged, and he sent his armies and destroyed those murderers and set their city on fire. Then he said to his slaves, 'The wedding is ready, but those who were invited were not worthy. Go therefore to the main highways, and as many as you find *there*, invite to the wedding feast.' Those slaves went out into the streets and gathered together all they found, both evil and good; and the wedding hall was filled with dinner guests.
>
> "But when the king came in to look over the dinner guests, he saw a man there who was not dressed in wedding clothes, and he said to him, 'Friend, how did you come in here without wedding clothes?' And the man was speechless. Then the king said to the servants, 'Bind him hand and foot, and throw him into the outer darkness; in that place there will be weeping and gnashing of teeth.' [14] For many are called, but few *are* chosen."

Our intimate relationship with the triune God serves as the foundation for our spiritual life. The Father desires that everybody celebrates this spiritual communion (2 Pt. 3:9). Jesus wants to participate at the exclusive and never-ending banquet. This invitation is extended to all people, but it is essential to wear the appropriate humility dress to enter the celebration. As Christian educators, we are messengers who proclaim the open invitation to come to the heavenly banquet. Teaching with the Holy Spirit's anointing proclaim that this invitation continues to be open to all. The same Holy Spirit also reminds us that we are God's children and, therefore, his special guests at the table (Rom. 8:16). What a pleasure and privilege to enjoy God's presence and to invite others to do the same!

### The Importance of Self-Care

Self-care is imperative because our ministry to others reflects our own spiritual life. Who we are is more important than what we do since the former shapes the later. Unfortunately, the culture around us fosters busyness and a logical consequence is the lack of personal care. Christian ministries and academic institutions tend to foster and reward this extreme activism and work without boundaries. I have taught in different educational contexts for several years and I have never heard an encouragement for professors to reduce their work and rest. On the contrary, busyness is perceived as a characteristic of dedication and persistence. Under these circumstances, most people struggle to survive their work and service activities, but not flourish in the abundant life that Jesus promises to his followers (John 10:10).

Consequently, rest and self-care are two extremely important elements in our spiritual life and our teaching ministry. We cannot love others if we do not love ourselves and we cannot teach something we are not. Work and ministry demands will never end, but our main calling is to proclaim the liberating message of God and to denounce everything that goes against God and others. We can only fulfill our calling when we let the Holy Spirit work in and through us.

The Christian life does not depend on our own efforts or dedication. In fact, in our strength the best we can do is to sin. The Christian life can only happen when the Holy Spirit takes control of our lives and we learn to walk in the Spirit (Gal. 5:16). A life that the Holy Spirit controls and directs produces the fruit of the Spirit: love, joy, peace, patience, kindness, goodness, faithfulness, gentleness, self-control (Gal. 5:22-23). In this way, the abundant life and the effective ministry are not based in what we do, but in what the Holy Spirit does through us. This reality liberates us from workaholism that stresses that true change only happens through our own efforts and forgets the transforming power of the Holy Spirit.

God is the one who is at work in us, both to will and to work according to his good pleasure (Phil. 2:13). As Christian leaders and educators we are special guests at the table with Jesus and invited to partner with the Holy Spirit. We are only the instruments that God uses according to his grace. A few years ago, I wrote some reflections about how marvelous is to be invited to partner with the Holy Spirit even though God does not need our help to accomplish his desires. These reflections serve as a conclusion to this chapter and as a call to rest and enjoy the privilege we have to partner with God under the power and anointing of the Holy Spirit.

## Lessons from a "Hinderer"[169]

I love spring time, but during this season I have to do something I regret and firmly believe it is the curse than comes along with the spring beauty. Next to the flowers, trees, and even the grass, weeds show up in my garden every year even if they are not welcome in my home. I really enjoy observing how the flowers grow, the trees, and the sound of the birds that visit our neighborhood. I consider mowing the yard a necessary evil and I would be more motivate to do it if the weeds were not there competing with the grass to see which one grows faster.

On one occasion, my son Darío taught me, without being conscious about it, an excellent lesson about my spiritual life, my relationship with the Lord, and my ministry. Darío was 2 and a half years old and he thought he was old enough to be independent and do his share at the household chores. Obviously, his advance age and development did not prevent him from seeking the love and care of his parents and to find refuge in his mom's arms.

Darío, just like all children, wants to be with his parents and help them in their different tasks. Therefore, at that time when I could not postpone pulling the weeds out from my yard anymore, Darío decided to help me and he told his mom that he would be my helper. I had to teach him the difference between the grass and the weeds and after a few minutes he was doing a decent job identifying them. However, it is impossible for a two-year-old to stay focused on any activity for several minutes. I constantly had to supervise that he would not do something wrong or that he would hurt himself. I also had to stop several times to play with him.

After more than an hour outside in the yard with Darío we had to go inside the house and he proudly told his mom that he had been a great help and that together we removed all weeds. In his own opinion, Darío was now a professional gardener and I should had been extremely grateful to receive his help. His face shone with satisfaction making perfectly clear this reality and I obviously thank him for his partnership during this difficult task.

The truth, however, was that we were not able to even finish half of the job with the weeds. If I had performed the task alone and my focus had been only the weeds, I am sure I could had finished the complete job in less than half the time. But my priority was my son and taking out the

[169] This conclusion is adapted from a blog article published at The Good Book Blog, the faculty blog at Talbot School of Theology. In Spanish, there is a play of words between "ayudante" (helper) and "estorbante" (hinderer) since both terms have a similar sound. https://www.biola.edu/blogs/good-book-blog/2015/lecciones-de-un-estorbante

163

weeds was just an excuse to spend time and play with him in the backyard. To be honest, my son was more my "hinderer" than my "helper." I could have done everything myself it would had been easier and faster. And yet, the smile on my son's face assured me that I made the best decision of all.

In the same way, the sovereign God of the universe does not need my help at all. Even though I consider of great value my ministry as a seminary professor and all the different tasks I perform here and in other countries, the truth is that God can accomplish his purposes with me or without me. In fact, most of the time he does it in spite of me. Although I consider important my education and service, in reality I am more God's "hinderer" than God's "helper."

Jesus promised that He and only He would edify His church (Matt. 16:18). The amazing reality about Christian ministry is to receive the sublime privilege of partnering with the omnipotent God through the Holy Spirit so the will of God will be done on earth as it is in heaven. God does not need us, but he wants to be with us and grants us the opportunity to help him in his work. Teaching with the Holy Spirit's anointing acknowledges that we are merely instruments in God's hands. Only the grace of God can explain such a distinct honor!

God desires to spend time with us because we are his children. Our relationship with God is essential for our identity and our actions. Our communion with God is more important than the work we do for him. Yes, of course we need to work hard, but God is the one who produces in us the will and the strength to work according to his will.

The time I spend playing with my children Darío and Salma does not compare to any class I teach or any book I write; It is much better. To be with them is also more important than any activity that we do together. In the same way, God loves us and he invites us to partner with the Holy Spirit. Do you accept his invitation?

# Conclusion

Óscar Merlo
Director, Center for the Study, of the Work and Ministry of the Holy
Spirit Today
Talbot School of Theology at Biola University

"What is the point of your education?" "Nothing!" replied the taxi driver in Cuba. I answered with the classic phrase, "that's interesting" because I did not want to be culturally insensitive. After twenty minutes of driving from the airport we finally reached the heart of the enchanting Havana. The next day, early in the morning I now find myself reflecting on this theme of "Anointed Teaching (AT)" from the lobby of Hotel Sevilla. In this context, we cannot ignore the influence of education to greatly advance the areas of science, business, religion and technology among others in Cuba as in the Americas, especially in the United States. Through education, knowledge in almost all scientific and academic fields has multiplied by leaps and bounds. According to David Russell Schilling, "at the end of World War II, knowledge doubled every 25 years."[170] Nowadays, according to the "Industry Tap" report, knowledge grows exponentially. For example, in the scientific industry of nanotechnology knowledge doubles every two years and in the medical field every 18 months. The report also indicates that on average, "human knowledge doubles every 13 months, and according to IBM, the 'Internet' led to the duplication of knowledge every 12 hours."[171]

Education is geopolitical essential for the personal, social, cultural and financial growth of global communities. For example, the taxi driver who transported me in Cuba was an expert in the field of mathematical calculus, but he earns his living as a driver because in this service he receives a better salary. The educational benefit in the case of the taxi driver is merely cognitive. Education provides an added human value. However, education is more than increasing human value and much more than obtaining educational equity. In the case of the taxi driver his secular education is not useful for him to have a job in his discipline and

---

[170] Gallivan, Michael J, Jim Eynon, and Arun Rai. 2003. *"The Challenge of Knowledge Management Systems."* Information Technology & People 16 (3): 326–52. doi:10.1108/09593840310489412.
[171] Schilling, Russell David. 2013. *Knowledge Doubling Every 12 Months, Soon to be Every 12 Hours. Industry* Tap.

also fails to provide avenues for personal or social holistic transformation. The situation of this man represents the one of many Latinos who throughout the Americas experience educational upsurge, but they are still trapped by very particular complex social and structural circumstances. Could it be that education, and in particular the art of teaching needs a component that produces other types of changes in individuals and societies? According to the proposal of this book, in order for education and teaching to produce transforming effects on human beings they must first receive "the Holy Spirit's anointing."

The thesis of this book is the presentation of a practical methodology rethought from the theology of the Holy Spirit, so that the teaching exercised in any discipline is much more effective in its task of promoting personal and social transformation. The union of the phrase "anointing of the Holy Spirit" with Christian educators and their discipline and methodology, pneumatologically merge to pursue greater *personal and social transformative effects*. These AT transforming effects first are experienced internally and then are externally reflected. This book calls them the five AT virtues; "Truth, faith, hope, love and joy." These virtues are first noticed in the life of the teacher and through the Holy Spirit's anointing, they also become a reality in the students. In addition, these virtues have a prophetic effect denouncing injustice in the word, promoting hope and righteousness. Let us continue examining these proposals that both authors make about "anointed teaching."

First, AT produces three concrete effects on human beings: "liberation, celebration and sustenance." Teachers with Anointed Teaching bring liberation. AT contributes in detaching the cognitive power in an individual and liberates him/her to grow in human value and in personal knowledge. AT is transformative and its effect must be holistic. That is, AT must affect the internal, external and social life of an individual. Therefore, the teaching, and specifically that which is exercised by Christian educators that are anointed with the power of the Holy Spirit (Acts 1: 2), encourage personal holistic transformation. By personal and holistic transformation, I mean the personal transformation of teachers and students who together are transformed to advance and celebrate the common good in our societies.

Are secular education and Christian teaching liberating, advancing and holistically celebrating the common human good? In my reading of Latin American contextual analysis minor advances have been made holistically, although good progress has been made cognitively! Secular education has other kinds of objectives that seek to provide primarily cognitive liberation, which are different from cognitive and behavioral agenda of Christian education anointed with the Holy Spirit. The epistemological agenda of both educations (secular / Christian) are different in many ways. Other questions come to mind at this point. Could Christian educators be more effective in their teaching to promote the liberation of people and social systems? Could it be that by integrating the Holy Spirit we can experience a higher degree of personal and social liberation and transformation through our teaching? What is lacking in Christian education and teaching to become more effective in the tasks of personal and social transformation? In other words, to continue fulfilling the transforming and liberating work of the Kingdom of God, it is urgent to reintegrate our teaching methodology with the Holy Spirit. We also need the Holy Spirit to integrate our orthodoxy with orthopraxis in our academic endeavors.

In this book the teacher is invited to consider the Holy Spirit as the Lord of teaching. Indeed, teaching given by Christians who invite the Holy Spirit to be part of their pedagogical methodology invite the Trinity (Father, Son and Holy Spirit) as the source that transforms and enlightens disciplines and individuals. This book provides theological-practical guidance with reference to the integration of the Holy Spirit into our various disciplines. Although its emphasis is primarily Christian education, the book is also be very useful for any educator.

The Holy Spirit must be the "distinguished professor" in our classrooms and he partners with us. The Holy Spirit is the one who imparts knowledge (orthodoxy) and the one who transforms the lives of students and teachers (orthopraxis). The Holy Spirit gives a fresh perspective to the application of what is being learned. Therefore, this combination of Spirit and knowledge, Spirit and lives, and Spirit and applications is a Pneumatology-Practical-Methodology of teaching that informs and sustains a new ecological educational system that this book calls "Anointed Teaching."

I consider this book written by distinguished scholars Robert W. Pazmiño and Octavio J. Esqueda, fundamental in the preparation of educators who seek to have a Pneumatological-Practical-Pedagogical framework to understand what it means to develop an education in the Spirit of Christ (anointed teaching with the Holy Spirit), as demonstrated by our Lord Jesus Christ in his teachings in Galilee, Samaria, Jerusalem and beyond.

Second, AT integrates the professor's "I / expert" with the life produced by the true specialist, the Holy Spirit. The Holy Spirit is the one who gives knowledge, wisdom and life. As educators we must move from the "I-expert" to be facilitators of the knowledge that is produced by the Spirit in our classrooms. This pedagogical task that depends on the Spirit of life is transformative and we must exercise it from a position of humility, without losing the academic rigor. We see this example in the life of our master Rabi Jesus Christ, as well as in the Prophets, Deborah, Daniel, Joshua, Priscilla, Paul and others.

Jesus Christ was anointed by the Holy Spirit of life to teach the truths of the kingdom of his Father and is the only one who can anoint our teaching with life (Mt 3:11). He taught us to be humble and practical in our teaching, and to recognize that we do not know everything. We are not the experts in our disciplines, but the real authority is the Holy Spirit (Mt 11:29). This challenge transforms the traditional dynamic from being the experts to become humble collaborators in the exercise of teaching as we become teaches who produce life. Humility is an indispensable characteristic given by the Holy Spirit to all, but it is especially important for scholars and professors who serve at universities, seminaries, Bible colleges, and Sunday schools.

Third, AT shares the peace and reconciliation of Christ as the bread that is served at the table of our communion with others. When Christian teaching aims to convey peace and reconciliation, it becomes a servant of the community as indicated by Pazmiño in the second part of this work. Here, we should ask ourselves these questions: What sustenance is Christian teaching providing in the formation of minds in our seminarians and university students? What is the bread that is being given and experienced; purely academic or is there something spiritual that when digested, produces personal and social transformation? The bread that AT offers must produce a personal and social holistic transformation (internal and external). By internal-external holistic transformation I mean one that encourages personal and social changes.

Firstly, AT fosters personal internal social transformation. Peter Kaufman defines personal social transformation as an interpersonal negotiation acquired by an individual and validated by others so that it is considered truly transformative.[172] In other words, the Holy Spirit through AT is transforming the lives of many people as we can see in these examples: The members of communist control committees in Cuba, which become followers of Christ in the underground churches are an example of personal social transformation. Ex-Cons and Sandinistas in Nicaragua who become pastors in Los Angeles California are another example. Or the paramilitaries in the maximum-security prisons in Colombia, receiving and ministering the love of Jesus to the ex-members of the FARC. Or, the ex-mara salvatrucha, who is now a tattooed Pastor who is teaching the gospel inside some of the most dangerous prisons in the world.

---

[172] Kaufman, Peter. *Sociological Quarterly.* Vol. 44, no. 3, pp. 481-504, summer 2003.

In this way, personal social transformation is happening. People are altering their social identity and this transformation is being validated by the "immediate other." Validated transformation is fostering new communities in spaces that are socially uncomfortable. These new communities are "Communities of the Spirit," as both Leonardo Boff in Brazil and theologian Oscar Garcia Johnson in Southern California call them. Teaching with the Holy Spirit's anointing produces these new communities. Just as we can see in Luke 6:18, AT is causing personal social transformation.

Secondly, the social transformation fostered by AT also has a social effect. Through AT, changes are taking place in the collective consciousness of society (local, state, national or global). In these social public spaces, AT is redefining reality through a process of collective consensus of certain evangelical communities. Therefore, we could affirm that AT exercised in the power of the Holy Spirit is refining the society conscience in several parts of the American continent. Cities that have reinvented themselves serve as examples of collective social transformations that have resulted in revitalized populations, economic prosperity and the restoration of civic pride.

Two examples of collective social transformation occurred in Medellin, Colombia after 1994 when the Pablo Escobar Cartel Wars' ended, and in the development of the economic revitalization of El Salvador. For social architects, education always plays a big role in these transformations. What social architects often forget is that the social transformation in these cities is preceded by the personal social transformation of individuals. The personal social transformation of individuals and society in this discussion is the work of the Holy Spirit in the life and society of the people produced via AT. When people are transformed personally (internally) by the power of the Holy Spirit, a social community transformation takes place. Such were the case of Medellín and El Salvador. In this way, AT is not only liberating, but transforming…it transforms the soul, it gives the bread of peace and reconciliation, and it socially transforms.

Finally, in third place, it is essential that the disciplines of education be rethought from a Pneumatological-Practical perspective. We educators ask ourselves, how can education and pedagogy be re-freshened or re-evaluated to be more practical and effective? The answer given in this book is that education must be integrated with the Holy Spirit. Our classes and our field of study should be open to the Holy Spirit. As teachers partner with the person of the Holy Spirit into their classroom and continue serving with academic rigor, they will experience a freshness in their teaching that is personal and socially transformative. To do this in humility is to open our lives to the fresh wind of the Spirit of Christ. Opening ourselves to the Spirit infuses our teaching methodologies with freshness and ignites the heart to fulfill through our disciplines the divine and cultural mandate of the Kingdom of God.

Robert W. Pazmiño and Octavio J. Esqueda have provoked us to (re) think the discipline of Christian teaching from a Pneumatological-Practical educational ecology. Both authors invite us as educators to seek an intimate closeness with the person of the Holy Spirit. He is the only one who produces changes (personal and social) that go beyond merely mental training. Without the transforming life of the Spirit, without "the anointing of the Spirit of Christ in teaching" we could become dry educators, who produce cognitive acquisition, but little personal and social transformation. May our teaching be anointed with the power of the Holy Spirit, may our lives be transformed and may our academic service reinvigorated.

*The Center for the Study of the Work and Ministry of the Holy Spirit Today* is a resource for students and scholars seeking a greater understanding and experience of the ongoing work of the Holy Spirit. Housed at Biola University's Talbot School of Theology, the center aims to produce biblically faithful resources that equip Christians to be transformed and empowered by the Spirit for the sake of the gospel.

### *Planned Resources*

### Global Leader-In-Residence
Each year, the center will invite an influential Christian leader to the campus to educate the community about the Holy Spirit's current work around the world.

### Spirit Empowerment "Poured Out" Chapels
Each month, the center will host evening Chapels titled "Poured Out," featuring guest speakers who will teach and lead students in inviting the Holy Spirit's renewal.

### Research Fellowship
Each semester, funding from the center will enable two professors to work collaboratively on a Spirit-focused research project.

### Academic Symposium
Every two years, the center will sponsor an academic conference featuring papers published by the faculty engaged in research.

### International Student Conference on Student Empowerment
Every two years, the center will house a gathering of students from around the world with the goal of advancing the gospel

## Collaborative Work with Biola Departments

As part of its ongoing efforts, the center will come alongside and enhance the existing efforts of departments across the university.

Contact:
Oscar Merlo, Director
*oscar.merlo@biola.edu*

Made in the USA
Columbia, SC
06 March 2019